A 6-SESSION BIBLE S
SINGLENESS & DA

CW01670398

Trusting God with Your Love Story

ERIN ELISE KIU

Trusting God with Your Love Story: A 6-Session Bible Study on Singleness & Dating
Copyright © 2022 by Erin Elise Kiu

All rights reserved. No part of this publication may be reproduced, distributed, or transmitted in any form or by any means, including photocopying, recording, or other electronic or mechanical methods, without the prior written permission of the publisher, except in the case of brief quotations embodied in critical reviews and certain other noncommercial uses permitted by copyright law.

Published by:
Erin Elise Kiu
San Diego, CA

Address all inquiries to:
Erin Elise Kiu
erinelisekiu@funandholy.com
www.funandholy.com

Paperback ISBN: 979-8-9866096-0-7
Library of Congress Control Number: 2022913410

Scripture quotations marked NLT are taken from the *Holy Bible,* New Living Translation, copyright © 1996, 2004, 2015 by Tyndale House Foundation. Used by permission of Tyndale House Publishers, Inc., Carol Stream, Illinois 60188. All rights reserved. Scripture quotations marked CSB are taken from The Christian Standard Bible. Copyright © 2017 by Holman Bible Publishers. Used by permission. Christian Standard Bible®, and CSB® are federally registered trademarks of Holman Bible Publishers, all rights reserved. Scripture quotations marked NIV are taken from THE HOLY BIBLE, NEW INTERNATIONAL VERSION®, NIV® Copyright © 1973, 1978, 1984, 2011 by Biblica, Inc.® Used by permission. All rights reserved worldwide. Scripture quotations marked ESV are taken from The Holy Bible, English Standard Version. ESV® Text Edition: 2016. Copyright © 2001 by Crossway Bibles, a publishing ministry of Good News Publishers. Used by permission. All rights reserved. Scripture taken from the New King James Version®. Copyright © 1982 by Thomas Nelson. Used by permission. All rights reserved. Scripture quotations marked MSG are taken from *THE MESSAGE,* copyright © 1993, 2002, 2018 by Eugene H. Peterson. Used by permission of NavPress. All rights reserved. Represented by Tyndale House Publishers, Inc.

Cover Design and Interior Layout: Fusion Creative Works
Author Photograph: Brooke Preece

Table of Contents

Introduction	5
Week 1: God's Design for Love & Marriage	7
Week 2: Finding Love Starts with Loving Yourself	41
Week 3: In the Waiting	75
Week 4: Baggage from the Past	109
Week 5: Single & Faithful	143
Week 6: God Writes the Best Love Stories	177
Note to Reader	211
Acknowledgments	215
Endnotes	217

Introduction

Have you ever noticed that the word 'dating' isn't in the Bible? People didn't date back then, but we live in a world where getting to know someone before marriage is a must. Introducing dating: an important stage for any woman looking to go from single to married.

But how do you date in a way that honors God? And how do you trust God when you've been praying for a husband for a long time? If you're fed up with the dating scene, or struggling to trust God with your love story, you're in the right place.

I didn't trust God with my love life until I was twenty-nine years old. For most of my twenties, I drank at bars and slept with men, hoping to find a husband. But after experiencing years of heartbreak, being ghosted on dating apps, and lots of Friday nights crying on my couch, I realized my approach to dating wasn't working. It would take a miracle to find my future husband. And I knew someone who specialized in miracles.

Surrendering my love life to God wasn't easy, but he showed me areas of my life that were holding me back. He gave me strength to let go of people from my past. And God restored every broken piece of my heart that men had shattered over the years. After a season of singleness and learning to trust God's best for my life, God brought me a godly husband who was more than I ever prayed for and imagined.

Navigating singleness, dating, and sex is tough, especially if you have a past like me. But God really does work all things for good, which is why I'm sharing my journey of singleness and dating with you.

As your sister in Christ, I don't want you to make the same dating mistakes I did. In this hookup culture, it's almost impossible to date and pursue a Christ-centered marriage. But when you trust God with your love story, all things are possible, including marrying a godly man.

If you want to discover the plans and future husband that God has for you, this is the Bible study for you.

How to Use This Bible Study

This Bible study is organized into a 6-week, 5-day study, where you'll study a different topic for six weeks for five days out of the week. Each day you'll have Bible verses to study, devotions, prayers, and questions to reflect on with each topic.

Study at your own pace. If you have less time each day, complete as much as your schedule allows. Use the weekends to catch up if you need to.

You can use a physical Bible or a Bible reading app to look up scriptures. If you decide to use a Bible on your phone, promise me you won't check Instagram until after you've done the study for the day :)

If you want to do this Bible study with a group or would like to access this study digitally, check out the group discussion guide and other resources at www.funandholy.com/biblestudy.

Meditating on the scriptures is key to making the most out of this study. But having an open heart as you seek God is the most important thing you need. I'll share how God spoke to me as I navigated singleness and dating, but nothing will compare to how God wants to speak to you personally. When you take the time to study his Word and commit your dating life to God through prayer, that's when you invite the Holy Spirit in to move.

Are you ready to discover God's best for your love life?

Grab a pen, your Bible, and a latte—let's do this.

With Love,

Erin Elise Kim

WEEK 1

God's Design for Love & Marriage

How God Defines Love

"This is how we have come to know love: He laid down his life for us."

1 John 3:16 CSB

Tears rolled down my face as I sat on the beach. I had moved to San Diego earlier that year and started dating Jake. We met while watching dolphins play in the ocean—it was like my own Nicholas Sparks novel in real life. In the past, I slept with guys in hopes they would want to date me. I didn't want to make the same mistake with Jake. But every time we hung out, one thing always led to another, and we ended up sleeping together. I hoped this would turn into something serious, but he told me he wasn't ready for a relationship.

I understood Jake wasn't my boyfriend. But every time I saw him, I secretly hoped that one day he would wake up and realize that he was falling in love with me. But that didn't happen.

I wiped another tear from my cheek. After six months of casually hooking up while not officially dating, we decided not to hang out or talk anymore. Jake made it clear he still wasn't ready for a relationship, and I knew I would continue to get hurt. Why hadn't I listened to him in the beginning? Why did I think we could "just be friends"? I felt naïve, thinking that Jake would eventually want to date me.

But there was one question that hurt the most. At this point, I attended church more and prayed to God daily. On that sunny day on the beach, I cried out to God, asking him the one question I had been wondering in my heart for years. "What's wrong with me, God? Why doesn't he love me? Why don't any guys love me or want to date me?"

I hung my head in my hands as the tears continued to fall. Jake was the same as all the other guys I had dated. They told me they liked me and cared about me, and sometimes they took me on romantic dates. But none of them wanted a serious relationship. As I surrendered my broken heart to God, he showed me why these guys didn't love me.

"My daughter," God whispered to my heart. "These guys don't love you because they don't know what love is. I am the source of love, and only I can show you what true love is."

If you're reading this Bible study, you most likely want to meet the guy you're supposed to marry and fall in love. But you have to understand how God defines love. How are you supposed to fall in love if you don't understand what love is?

Before we dive in to the study, I want you to be honest with yourself. How would you define love in your own words? What does love look like in a romantic relationship?

You've probably heard the Bible verse in John 3:16 before. The NIV translation says, "For God so loved the world that he gave his one and only Son". But God has a lot more to say about what love is supposed to look like.

Read 1 John 3:16-18 and 1 John 4:7-21. In your own words, how does God describe what love is?

God himself is love, and love comes from God. 1 John 3:18 illustrates that we are called to love in action and in truth, and not just word or speech. The MSG version says, "Let's not just talk about love; let's practice real love." Basically, we can say we love someone all we want, but if we don't show that love by our actions, our words mean nothing.

Just like his Word says, God models what love is through his actions. In 1 John 3:16 and 1 John 4:10, God tells us that love is also a sacrifice. He showed this love by sacrificing his only son to die on the cross for us. In Romans 5:8, the Bible emphasizes this sacrificial love again. "But God showed his great love for us by sending Christ to die for us while we were still sinners." (NLT)

Love is a sacrifice—where we sacrifice our own needs or wants out of love for the other person. Sacrificial love is also known as *agape* love, where we serve the other person unconditionally without expecting anything in return.

God has more to say about love in 1 Corinthians 13:4-6. Pastors and officiants cite these scriptures at weddings, but I want you to focus on what God is trying to tell you about love.

Read 1 Corinthians 13:4-6. What stands out to you about love in these scriptures?

Sometimes, this definition of love seems impossible. How can anyone be all of these things? Jesus models this type of love so well in the gospels, but this definition of love teaches us a lot about how to love others.

The NLT version of 1 Corinthians 13:7 says, "Love never gives up, never loses faith, is always hopeful, and endures through every circumstance." Love is a promise to be there for someone in sickness and in health. Love is deciding in advance to be there in both the good times and the bad.

In summary, we've learned the following about God's definition of love:

1. Love is sacrificial, or sacrificing your own wants and needs to love and serve the other person
2. Love is not self-seeking
3. Love doesn't keep a record of wrongs or past mistakes
4. Love never gives up and endures through every circumstance
5. We are called to love through our actions, not just with our words

Understanding God's definition of love is essential in romantic relationships. If we don't understand love in the way God intended it, we won't be able to receive or give true love. And since God is love, we cannot truly love others without experiencing God himself.

Go back to your definition of love that you wrote at the beginning of this lesson. How does your definition compare to God's definition of love?

When I was looking for love, I never would have defined love as being willing to sacrifice my own needs for the other person. When I cried out to God, asking him why nobody loved me, I was looking for romance, passion, and for a man to take me to fancy Italian restaurants. I wanted an intense connection with someone where we couldn't keep our hands off each other. And I wanted to talk about anything and everything.

My definition of love was based on a physical connection with someone, and how much fun we had while talking to each other. But after God revealed his definition of love, I finally understood why none of the guys I had dated in the past loved me. Their definition of love was flawed, just like mine was. They couldn't love me in the way I wanted because they didn't understand the love that can only come from God.

But where did we go wrong? How did our definition of love get so distorted from how God defines it? A big part to understanding love is understanding what love isn't. Tomorrow, we'll discuss the world's definition of love, and how it doesn't measure up to God's definition.

Pray the prayer below, or pray what God is putting on your heart.

God, thank you for showing me what true love is by sending Jesus to die for my sins. Open my heart and eyes during this Bible study to see love and relationships in the way you intended. In Jesus' name, amen.

Breaking Up with the World's Definition of Love

***"Trust in the Lord with all your heart,
and do not rely on your own understanding;
in all your ways know him, and he will make your paths straight."***

Proverbs 3:5-6 CSB

I used to believe that I needed to have sex with a guy in order for him to want to date me. As a teenager, I read *Cosmopolitan* magazine and watched romantic comedies. Culture taught me I had to use my body to get a guy to like me. Ever since high school, my friends and I started hooking up with guys, thinking that this was the way to find true love and eventually a husband.

Fast forward to my twenties, my friends and I continued dressing up in revealing outfits, hoping to meet a guy at the bar. It worked at first, because we realized that looking a certain way got attention from men. I felt desired and wanted, which made me feel beautiful. But then I realized that this approach to dating only made me feel worse about myself. I went home with men, excited that it could be the start of something new, but realized they only texted me for sex. All these sexual relationships left me feeling lonelier, broken, and rejected. I didn't feel loved at all.

God revealed these men couldn't love me because they didn't know what love was. But God also showed me I had been believing lies about what love was supposed to look like. I had been letting culture define love instead of God, and I had been looking for love in all the wrong places.

Yesterday, we discussed God's definition of love. Today, we're discussing what love isn't by exposing some of the biggest myths women believe about love. We'll also discuss how to use God's definition as a filter against any beliefs you have about love.

Myth #1: Sex by itself is love

Read 1 Thessalonians 4:3-8. What does God say about our bodies?

When I surrendered my love life to God, the first thing God taught me was that sex by itself is not love. Sex can be a way for a husband and wife to express love in marriage, but sex can't be used to find love. The MSG translation of 1 Thessalonians 4:4-5 says, "Learn to appreciate and give dignity to your body, not abusing it, as is so common among those who know nothing of God."

Culture tells women that the way to get a man's attention is through sex appeal. Magazines claim that sex is one of the most important aspects of a relationship. But God showed me I was abusing my body, and that having sex outside of marriage only led to lust.

Myth #2: Lust is love

Women are looking for love in a lustful world. But we can't use sex to find love. Using sex to find love only leads to lust, and lust is not love. But how do you know the difference between love and lust?

Merriam-Webster[1] defines lust as a strong feeling of sexual desire or a strong desire for something. In 1 John 2:16, the Bible tells us that lust is not from God. "For everything in the world—the lust of the flesh, the lust of the eyes, and the pride in one's possessions—is not from the Father, but is from the world." (CSB)

Lust is not from God. It's a spirit from the devil that's at work to distort how God designed love and sex. People experiencing lust are often consumed by the other person. They may experience a strong desire to sleep with them, or find that they cannot stop thinking about the person. Lust can also be an uncontrolled sexual desire, where the person cannot stop themselves from having sex, or cannot stop themselves from watching porn.

We live in a world where lust fuels romantic relationships. But God intended for romantic relationships to be based on love. If you're experiencing lust, we'll talk more about how to get freedom from lust in week 4 of this Bible study.

Myth #3: Love is based on a feeling

Many people rely on their feelings to determine if they love someone, and express their love by their strong desire to be with them. But just because you have intense feelings for someone doesn't mean it's love. Let's see what God says about relying on our feelings or our desires.

Read and write out Jeremiah 17:9.

Read Galatians 5:16-18 and summarize in your own words below.

In Proverbs 3:5-6, God tells us not to rely on our own understanding, but to trust in the Lord with all our heart. Feelings can change, and if we followed our feelings for every decision we made, we would make a lot of poor decisions. Do you remember the definition of love from 1 Corinthians 13 about not giving up? God says that love never gives up and endures through every circumstance. The problem with relying on our feelings to define love is that our feelings can change, and some days we may not feel like loving our spouse.

To illustrate, imagine a 70-year-old man visits his wife, who has Alzheimer's disease, in the nursing home. If you've read or seen *The Notebook*, remember how Noah loved Allie when they were old. Allie is in a nursing home, not able to remember her husband Noah, yet Noah shows up every day to read to her. Do you think Noah felt like reading to Allie every day, when she didn't remember who he was? It probably broke his heart, but he chose to show up every day out of love.

When a couple's love is based on a commitment to be there for the other person, it's a beautiful representation of unconditional love. Feelings can fade, but true love is a commitment to be there no matter what.

God created us to have emotions, feelings, and desires, but not every desire is from God. In Galatians 5:16-18, the Bible talks about how the desires of our flesh and our Spirit are at war with each other. Our flesh, or our bodies, may desire something that is not from God. Just because you feel like dating someone doesn't mean it's from God. And just because you feel like you're in love, doesn't mean it's godly love. For example, you may be attracted to a married man, or have the desire to watch porn. Or maybe you feel attracted to a woman. These desires are not from God. They are from the devil and are most likely a result of lust or perversion at work in your life.

According to *The Meaning of Marriage*[2], by Timothy Keller, one reason the divorce rate is so high is because people get divorced after they "fall out of love". The intense feeling of love wears off after a period of time in marriage. When couples don't feel this strong in-love-feeling anymore, they think they don't love each other and get divorced.

But godly love is not based on an intense feeling of being in love. While some days you may feel like you are passionately in love with your spouse, love is choosing to be there for the other person, regardless of how you are feeling.

Myth #4: Love can be earned

God calls us to show our love for others in action, but we can't earn love from others based on the things we do. Just like God loves us unconditionally, where there is nothing we can do to earn God's love, he calls us to love others for who they are. When you try to get someone to love you based on what you can do for them, the relationship is based on performance—not love. Over time, this creates a works-based foundation for love which was not God's design.

If a man wants to marry you because you'll make the perfect housewife, this should not be the foundation of your marriage. It's important to understand how you'll contribute to the household, but love should not be based on what you do. Love should be based on who you are.

What other lies have you believed about love? What did you think was love that really wasn't?

What influenced your definition of love? Who or what shaped how you defined love?

The world's definition of love is based on an intense feeling or emotion. Passion, attraction, and lust fuel the search for love in this world. But God says that love is a sacrifice that is put in action, whether or not you feel it. Love is choosing to be there for someone on their best and worst days. Sacrifice, commitment, and forgiveness fuels God's definition of love.

How are we supposed to bridge the gap between the world's definition and God's definition of love? Does this mean we shouldn't have passion or chemistry with our spouse? God created marriage, and he also created sex. As we see in Song of Solomon, God wants a husband and wife to experience passion in marriage. But when we focus on serving our spouse out of love, this creates a deeper love than passion and chemistry could ever provide.

Relationships built on God's definition of love allows each person to feel fully known and loved. The feeling of being loved despite your flaws? It doesn't even compare to the feeling of love through sex.

When my husband and I were engaged, we were waiting until our wedding night to have sex. Since we hadn't gotten physical yet, I realized my husband loved me for me, and not because of my body. In other relationships, I tried to feel loved through sex, but realizing that my husband loved me for me? It was one of the most beautiful examples of love that I've ever experienced.

Pray the prayer below, or pray what God is putting on your heart.

God, thank you for showing me what love is through Jesus Christ. I surrender the lies I've believed about love, and I renounce these lies. Thank you for continuing to show me what love looks like. And thank you for bringing me a man who will love me like Jesus loves me. In Jesus' name, amen.

The Purpose of Marriage

"Husbands, love your wives, just as Christ loved the church and gave himself for her to make her holy, cleansing her with the washing of water by the word."

Ephesians 5:25-26 CSB

I tried not to cry as I gazed out the plane window. I was coming home from a work trip that required me to travel across the country, and I was sick of not having someone to enjoy all my travels with. Part of me felt grateful that I got to fly to exciting places like Orlando, Colorado, and New York, but I wanted a boyfriend to explore with.

I wanted someone who enjoyed hiking, and a man to share French toast with during brunch. Someone who knew how to relax on the beach, but was also up for an adventure. Basically, I wanted someone to do all my favorite activities with.

I avoided looking at the couple holding hands across the aisle from me on the plane. Instead, I prayed God would bring me someone to travel to romantic resorts with. When would I get to experience my dream honeymoon in the Maldives?

As I prayed for my future husband and surrendered my desires to God, God showed me that marriage was so much more than having someone to enjoy life with. Today, we are discussing why God created marriage, and the purpose of getting married.

Before we begin today's lesson, answer this question. Why do you want to get married one day?

Maybe you are sick of spending Friday nights alone. Or maybe you're fed up with roommates who eat all your food, and you can't wait until you have a husband to cuddle on the couch with. If you've committed to purity and been celibate for a while, maybe you want to get married so you can have sex again. (Girl, I've been there!)

Understanding why you want to get married will determine if you are ready to become a wife. Marriage is a responsibility, and it's important to make sure you want to get married for the right reasons.

Read Genesis 1:28 and Genesis 2:18-24. In these scriptures, we witness the first marriage ever between Adam and Eve. What do you learn about God's purpose for marriage in these scriptures?

In the first few chapters in the Bible, God shows us a few reasons he created marriage. God calls Adam and Eve to be fruitful and to multiply, to fill the Earth and to govern it, and to reign over the animals of the Earth. When you hear the phrase "be fruitful and multiply", you may think of reproduction. And yes, having babies is one purpose of marriage. But being fruitful and multiplying in marriage is more than just making a cute mini version of yourself.

Marriage is a ministry and a responsibility to steward and multiply what God has given you. Each individual family has a responsibility to steward their own household and family, but God calls us to steward marriage and be fruitful in all aspects of life.

God also points out the importance of companionship in marriage. I love how God looked at Adam and realized, "It is not good for man to be alone." God knew that a man would need a woman in his life—someone to do life with and someone to be his helper.

In Ecclesiastes 4:9-12 CSB, it tells us again that companionship is important to God. "Two are better than one" because if either person falls, his companion can lift him up. God also points out that two people can resist someone who tries to overpower them. He concludes that "A cord of three strands is not easily broken."

If you are single right now reading this, I hope this brings you peace. Companionship is one of God's purposes for marriage. It is normal to want to spend your life with someone. God does not want you to be alone, and he knows that a husband and wife in marriage are more powerful working together.

In Genesis 2:24, God also tells us that marriage unites a husband and wife into one. But what does this mean and why is it important? Mark 10:9 CSB says, "What God has joined together, let no one separate." God intended for marriage to be forever. Marriage is a permanent, covenant-type of relationship that is not meant to be broken.

God has already told us a lot about the purpose of marriage through these scriptures. Now, I want you to turn to Ephesians 5 in your Bible. No other passage in the Bible explains the purpose of marriage like this one.

Read Ephesians 5:22-33. What analogy or comparison does God use to illustrate how a husband should love his wife?

Comparing a husband and wife's relationship to Jesus and the church is significant. God tells us that marriage is supposed to model the type of love that Jesus has for the church. Think back to day 1 where we talked about how God defines love. Remember how God's love is sacrificial?

In Ephesians 5, God tells us that this type of sacrificial love between a husband and wife is supposed to point others to the sacrificial love of Jesus. In marriage, husbands are to love their wives like Jesus loves the church. Husbands are called to lay down their lives for their wives out of love. But is this type of love even possible in today's culture?

After years of getting my heart broken, I doubted whether this type of love existed. How could any man love me the way Jesus loved me?

As I write this Bible study, I've been married for almost two years. I've witnessed several examples of sacrificial love from my husband Jeff. He did the dishes when it was my turn, he cooked dinner for my friends when I hosted girl's night, and he held me up when I was too sick to walk by myself. But I'll never forget the moment where I first experienced the Ephesians 5 type of love. We were engaged, and I had just received my test results from a Pap smear. My results were positive again for HPV. At this point, I had already repented from my sexual lifestyle, and I hadn't had sex in over a year. As I debated whether to tell Jeff, shame and fear overtook me. What would my fiancé think of me? Would he think I was tainted goods? One night before I left his house, I couldn't keep it to myself any longer. I told him about the test results. I apologized for bringing this into our marriage and told him how sorry I was for sleeping with other men.

Jeff tilted my chin up so I would look at him. Instead of judging me or looking at me with disgust, his eyes were full of compassion and mercy. He prayed for me to be healed, and he prayed against the shame from my past. A few tears escaped down his cheeks, and he said, "I see you how Jesus sees you. Forgiven and white as snow. Your sins have already been forgiven, and I don't judge you for your sins either."

We both cried and held each other for what seemed like hours. It was that moment when I first experienced love from a man in the way Jesus intended. Just like Jesus, Jeff didn't hold my past against me. Instead, he declared God's Word over me. Now that we're married, we're able to enjoy sex in the way God intended, without the shame from my past.

My friend, I don't know what type of men you've dated in the past, but I pray God brings you a husband who will love you like Jesus loves you. I pray God heals your heart from any abuse or pain from the past. And I pray God shows you what the love of Christ looks like in a relationship.

Pray the prayer below, or pray what God is putting on your heart.

God, thank you for creating marriage and for showing me what marriage is supposed to look like. I pray you bring me a husband who will love me like Jesus loves me. I pray you will be the center of our marriage, and that together, we will point others to the sacrificial love of Jesus Christ. In Jesus' name, amen.

Every Marriage Has a Mission

"But as for me and my house, we will serve the Lord."

Joshua 24:15 ESV

I rolled my eyes as I opened another Christmas card displaying the perfect family photo on a beach. As if the photo wasn't enough, my friend also described everything they had accomplished that year. I wanted to be happy for my married friends, but this Christmas card was a reminder of how single I still was. And it reminded me how much I hadn't accomplished yet. Not only did I not have a husband, but I also didn't have the dream house, the fancy cars, the dog, the kids in matching plaid pajamas, or the family vacations to Disney to boast about.

As I prayed that night, I knew the bitterness in my heart wasn't healthy. But I was fed up with how the world defined success. Why did culture view married women as more successful? When I got Christmas cards like this, it was like putting fuel on a fire, and it made me question the purpose of marriage. Was the purpose of marriage to achieve certain milestones to prove that you had made it? It seemed like life was a constant competition to have and do more, while having the perfect home and family to brag about.

As a single woman, how would I ever measure up to this standard? Deep down, I wanted a husband to take long walks on the beach with while we walked our dog and held our baby. But was marriage really all about keeping up with my neighbor, and accumulating bigger and better possessions?

Today, we're studying how God uses marriage to build his kingdom and make a difference in this world. I refer to this concept as "missional marriages." To illustrate what a missional marriage looks like, we're going to study Mary and Joseph in the Bible. Even though you may study these scriptures every Christmas as you reflect on the birth of Jesus, today we will focus on Mary and Joseph's marriage, and how God used their marriage to bring our Savior into this world.

Read Luke 1:26-38. What did the angel say to Mary that shows she was chosen by God?

You probably know how an angel appeared to Mary and told her she would get pregnant and give birth to Jesus as a virgin. The angel told Mary she found favor with God, showing us that God had chosen her to birth the Messiah. Even if the angel didn't tell Mary that she was chosen, we know that whoever God chose to give birth to Jesus was chosen for a reason. But what about Joseph? How come people don't talk about his role?

Read Matthew 1:18-25 and Matthew 2:13-23. How did the angel appear and speak to Joseph?

What role did Joseph have as Jesus' father in these passages?

God appeared to Joseph multiple times through dreams. God first sent an angel to Joseph to confirm that the baby inside Mary had been conceived by the Holy Spirit. After Jesus was born, God spoke to Joseph, not Mary, to protect Jesus from King Herod.

A lot of sermons talk about how Mary was chosen, but have you ever noticed that Joseph was also chosen? Mary played an instrumental role in bringing Jesus into this world, but God used Joseph to protect and watch over Jesus. Just like Mary, God chose Joseph because he knew Joseph would obey him. Mary and Joseph did not have the engagement and wedding they had planned. But they were both selected by God to fulfill a mission as Jesus' earthly parents.

Just like Mary and Joseph, God has a plan and purpose for each one of our lives, including our marriages. We learned yesterday that marriage is supposed to represent the sacrificial love that Jesus has for the church. God also uses marriage to build his kingdom and to make a difference in this world.

A few years ago in Hawaii, Pastor Jentezen Franklin preached a message about missional marriages at a conference. He talked about the importance of God's people coming together and forming strong, godly marriages for such a time as this. When God calls two people into a marriage, he has a call and an assignment for them.

Marriage isn't just about what God wants to do for you. It's about what he wants to do through your life, and how he wants to use your marriage to impact the lives around you.

What purpose or calling has God given you? How important is it that your spouse supports you in this mission?

Since God's purpose for each one of our lives is different, his purpose and plans for our marriages will also be unique. God may call both you and your husband to do ministry, or he may call you to run a business together. For example, John and Lisa Bevere's ministry, Messenger International, is one of my favorite examples of a missional marriage that I respect and admire. God has given them both the gift to preach and teach men and women around the world. Their marriage and ministry remind me what's possible when a husband and wife obey the call of God on their lives.

While God calls some couples to do ministry or business together, not all couples will have the same role as their spouse. God may call you and your husband to different jobs, and he may call one of you to stay home and raise kids when you start a family.

If you have the desire to be a stay-at-home mom and raise kids to serve the Lord, don't underestimate the importance of this role. Raising godly children in today's culture is difficult, and many people argue that raising kids to walk in God's ways is the most important job you could have. At my church in San Diego, we prophesy parents are raising "giant slayers" for such a time as this, because their kids will grow up to destroy the works of the devil in their generation.

As you reflect on what your marriage will look like, it's important to keep in mind that a missional marriage will look different for every couple. Your mission may also fluctuate as seasons change and your kids grow up. For example, both my mom and mother-in-law left their careers to be a stay-at-home mom when they had kids. After their kids went to school, they then pursued jobs outside the home again.

As I write this study, my husband and I serve together on our welcome team at church, and we also have a heart to help single men and women prepare for godly marriages. My husband still has a full-time job in sales, and I write full-time. While we have different jobs as we serve God, we work together and support each other for the overall mission that God has for our lives.

What examples of missional marriages do you see in couples around you? How do they serve God through their marriage?

Marriage is more than living happily ever after in a big house while raising kids and going on family vacations. God wants to use marriage for his glory, and to build his kingdom and make a difference in this world. Two are better than one, and you and your husband will accomplish more than you can imagine.

Pray the prayer below, or pray what God is putting on your heart.

God, thank you for giving me purpose for my life and for my future marriage. I pray that my future husband and I will support each other's purpose, and that we will leave a legacy for you in this world. Open my heart and eyes to see how you are using marriage to point others to Christ. In Jesus' name, amen.

Equally Yoked in Marriage

"Do not be unequally yoked with unbelievers. For what partnership has righteousness with lawlessness? Or what fellowship has light with darkness?"

2 Corinthians 6:14 ESV

Growing up, my mom always told me how important it was to date and marry someone who shared my faith. But this became less important to me over time. I had always believed that God existed, and I wanted a guy who shared my faith so we could raise our kids to know Jesus. But none of the guys I met in my twenties ever talked about God, so I thought it wasn't a big deal.

I wasn't going to wait to find a man who believed in God when I could barely find a decent guy as it was. If a guy had everything else I was looking for, his lack of faith wouldn't be a deal breaker. But as I got serious about establishing a personal relationship with God, he showed me the importance of reading and obeying the Bible. God showed me that his commands weren't meant to be a burden or a bunch of rules. They were intended to protect me for my own good.

As I dug into God's Word, I wondered what God said about dating someone outside of the faith. What does the Bible say about dating and marrying a guy who isn't a Christian? Today, we're studying whether it's okay for Christians to date or marry nonbelievers.

Read 2 Corinthians 6:14-18.

In the ESV translation, verse 14 says, "Do not be unequally yoked with unbelievers." The NLT translation says, "Don't team up with those who are unbelievers." Both translations question what partnership righteousness has with wickedness and how light can live with darkness. The NLT translation raises the question, "What harmony can there be between Christ and the devil?"

But what does unequally yoked mean and why is this a big deal in marriage? These scriptures in 2 Corinthians 6 are most often used to describe why a Christian should only date and marry other Christians. But it's important to understand what unequally yoked means. Many people in the Bible were farmers, so they used a yoke to plow a field. A yoke is a wooden bar or frame that joins two animals together at the head or neck to work together. For example, a yoke joined a pair of horses, so they could work side by side to pull a plow.

In a farming sense, it was important for animals to be equally yoked so they could accomplish the task at hand. If a horse was larger or stronger than the other horse, they would not get as much work done. Imagine a racehorse yoked to a pony. Do you think they would work well together? The pony would hold the racehorse back from achieving its full potential.

In marriage, God wants a husband and wife to be equally yoked so they can accomplish what God has called them to do for his kingdom. In a world of darkness and distractions, God knows it's hard enough for Christians to focus on him. He doesn't want an unbelieving spouse to hold the believing spouse back in marriage. You are one of God's most prized racehorses, and he doesn't want you with a pony. I don't care how cute the pony is. A man who doesn't follow Jesus will only hold you back in life.

God warns his people about marrying someone who doesn't walk in his ways several times in the Bible. When God gave Moses the Ten Commandments, God reminded Moses and his people not to intermarry with foreign wives. The reason? "And they will seduce your sons to commit adultery against me by worshiping other gods." (Exodus 34:16 NLT)

God does not want his people worshipping other gods or wanting anything in life more than him. When a Christian marries a non-Christian, the nonbelieving spouse will tempt them to drift from God's ways. God warns his people again in Deuteronomy 7 not to intermarry right before his people enter the Promised Land. In Deuteronomy 7:3-4 NLT, God says, "Do not let your daughters and sons marry their sons and daughters, for they will lead your children away from me to worship other gods."

Notice how God points out that their children will be tempted to worship other gods. God warns us that not only will we ourselves be tempted to stray from God if we marry a nonbeliever, but that our children will be led astray as well. Think of all the controversial beliefs that culture is teaching children. When it comes to abortion, knowing their identity as a man or woman, and whether it's okay to have premarital sex, do you want a husband who will teach your children God's truth? Or do you want a spouse that will influence your kids to stray from God's Word?

Like we learned earlier this week, God has a plan and purpose for your marriage. He calls you to be fruitful and to multiply with your spouse, and he wants you to use your marriage for his glory. This includes raising children that love God and walk in his ways, not raising kids who will distort God's truth and live in sin.

By yourself, you can accomplish a lot for God's kingdom. With a godly spouse, you probably think you can accomplish two times as much. But in an article inspired by best-selling author Jim Stovall (timmaurer.com)[3], I heard a message about draft horses that illustrates the power of a Christ-centered marriage.

Draft horses are muscular horses used to pull heavy objects. One draft horse can pull a load of up to 8,000 pounds. You'd think that two draft horses of the same size could pull double the weight. But two draft horses working together can actually pull three times as much. And if the horses are used to working with each other, they can pull 32,000 pounds, which is four times the amount either horse could pull by themselves.

When you marry someone who loves God, it allows God to multiply what you can accomplish for his kingdom. God doesn't want a nonbelieving spouse holding you back. Marriage requires both spouses working together, and God doesn't want your husband pulling you away from Christ.

Even if you're just dating someone who doesn't have a relationship with God, he'll still tempt you to drift away from God's Word. For example, a guy may not understand why it's important to wait until marriage to have sex. Even if he respects your decision to wait, he may pressure you to give in over time.

But what if you are strong spiritually on your own? What if there's no way you would ever turn from God? In 2 Corinthians 6:14-16 NLT, it says, "What harmony can there be between Christ and the devil?" If you marry a man who doesn't follow God, you are essentially marrying a man who follows the ways of the devil. In Ephesians 2:2, it says that those who disobey God follow the ruler of this world, who is the devil.

No matter how strong you are spiritually, God does not want the devil to have control over any part of your life, including your marriage. As we can see through these scriptures, God clarifies his people are to only marry someone who loves the Lord. And since you date someone with the goal of finding someone to marry, it would not be wise to date a guy who doesn't have a relationship with God.

Describe in your own words why it's important to date and marry a guy who loves the Lord.

God wants you to be equally yoked in marriage, but how do you know if you're equally yoked? If a guy says he's a Christian, is that good enough?

If you've been in the dating scene long enough, you've probably realized that just because someone says they believe in God doesn't always mean they love God in their heart. And just because you meet a cute guy in church doesn't mean you should date him.

He could have closed down the club last night, and showed up to church last minute.

Just because a guy says he's a Christian on his dating profile does not mean he's a true follower of Christ. To determine if you are equally yoked with someone, it's important to make sure you are on the same level spiritually in your relationship. Even though a guy goes to church, you could still be unequally yoked if he's not as spiritually mature as you.

For example, you could be unequally yoked if you spend time with God daily, and a guy only wants to spend time with God at church on Sundays. You could also be unequally yoked if you live by God's Word in the Bible, but your boyfriend doesn't read or follow what God's Word says. You could also be unequally yoked if one of you lives by the Holy Spirit, and the other person does not follow or rely on the Holy Spirit at all.

Does this mean that you shouldn't date a new believer, or a guy who is recently saved? Or what if you meet a guy who isn't a Christian, but he's open to pursuing a relationship with Jesus?

Only God can tell you whether you should date someone. But if a guy is open to pursuing God, his willingness and desire to grow in his walk with Christ is most important. A guy may not be as strong as you spiritually, but if he's doing the work to seek God on his own, then that's a good sign. However, if a guy goes to church to make you happy but isn't pursuing his own relationship with Christ, then you will be unequally yoked.

Can you still date a guy in hopes that he will turn to Jesus? When I studied what the Bible said about dating nonbelievers, I was dating a guy, Jake, who had no interest in pursuing God. When God convicted me through these scriptures, I started bawling. Even if Jake wanted to date me, we couldn't be together. I wanted a boyfriend, but I loved God more, and I wanted to obey and respect God's commands in the Bible. I knew God was telling me to let Jake go, but I continued to hold on to the relationship. What if he changed his mind? What if I could be a good influence in his life, and Jake would want to come to church with me?

I continued seeing Jake for a few more months, and God only confirmed what he had already told me. After more pain and heartbreak, Jake only brought me further away from God's plans.

If you're single, missionary dating is not wise, where you date someone hoping they will give their life to Jesus or become a Christian. Single women have a responsibility to treat men with respect and to share the gospel as they feel led, but this does not mean you should date someone in order to lead them to Christ.

After I stopped talking to Jake, I met other men who didn't have a relationship with God. If they asked for my number, I was honest and told them I only dated men that loved God. If they had questions about my faith, I answered them. But I never dated someone hoping they would turn to Jesus along the way.

If you're reading this and are married to a man who isn't walking with God, this does not apply to you. While God still wants his people to be equally yoked in marriage, he has specific instructions for those who are already married and find themselves unequally yoked (see 1 Corinthians 7:12-16).

You've learned a lot about God's design for marriage this week, and I want to ask you a serious question. Will you make the commitment to only date and marry a guy who loves the Lord?

Pray the prayer below, or pray what God is putting on your heart.

God, I believe you have a man of God out there for me. I want to be equally yoked in marriage, and I want to date a man who has a relationship with Jesus. Lord, give me the strength to only date someone who loves you with all his heart. In Jesus' name, amen.

WEEK 1 REFLECTION

God's Design for Love & Marriage

Take some time to reflect and look back at how God spoke to you this past week. Journal your thoughts below, and consider answering the following questions:

- What key takeaways or revelations did you have this week?
- Which scriptures or Bible verses stuck out to you?
- What are you going to do differently moving forward?

WEEK 1 REFLECTION

WEEK 2

Finding Love Starts with Loving Yourself

Worth So Much More

"So if anyone purifies himself from anything dishonorable, he will be a special instrument, set apart, useful to the Master, prepared for every good work."

2 Timothy 2:21 CSB

Have you ever replayed an event in your mind, wishing that you could go back and do things differently? After Jake and I stopped talking, I couldn't stop rehearsing the highs and lows of our time together. I wished I had never slept with him in the first place, and I should have ended things sooner.

I couldn't get back the time I had wasted with Jake. The more I reflected on past relationships, the more frustrated I got. Why did I make the same mistakes over and over? I had always wanted a serious relationship, but I continued giving my body away to men. Why did these men think it was okay to treat me like a toy? I thought I was wife material, but men just wanted to hook up with me. When would I meet someone who would actually want to date me?

As I prayed and journaled my frustrations to God, he revealed another reason that was preventing me from experiencing the love story that I wanted. Not only had I failed to understand what love was supposed to look like, but I had failed to understand my own worth. God showed me I was trying to find my worth in men and sex, instead of discovering my worth in Jesus Christ.

Today, we're discussing how Jesus defines your worth. If you want to be loved by a man, you have to learn to first love yourself. The key to loving who God created you to be starts with understanding how much you're worth to Jesus.

Read Psalm 139:13-18. Which scriptures or words speak to your heart ?

Whenever I need a reminder of what God says about me, I let the words of Psalm 139 wash over my heart. God loves and delights in you so much that he knew the plans he had for you before you were even born. He formed you in your mother's womb, and you are wondrously and remarkably made. You are so precious to God, my friend, that his thoughts about you outnumber the grains of sand on the beach!

God shows you how special you are to him in Psalm 139, but he has a lot more to say about you. Look up the following scriptures and write what God says about you in each verse. I included the first verse for you to get started.

Ephesians 2:10

"For we are God's masterpiece. He has created us anew in Christ Jesus, so we can do the good things he planned for us long ago." (NLT)

Jeremiah 1:5

2 Timothy 2:20-21

Isaiah 43:4

In week 1, we talked about how Jesus showed his love for us by sacrificing himself on the cross. Jesus sacrificed himself to save us, but it's important to understand how much you are worth to him. In 1 Corinthians 6:20, it says that we were purchased at a price. In Romans 5:8, it tells us that while we were still sinners, Jesus died for us.

My friend, you are worth dying for. Jesus loves you so much that he sacrificed his life on the cross for your life. God chose you and set you apart before you were born. He considers you his masterpiece, his work of art. You are so precious to God. He loves you so much that he considers you to be a gold vessel, set apart for honorable use.

To illustrate how much you are worth to God, I want you to imagine that you are about to purchase your dream pair of shoes. Maybe you're thinking of a pair of Christian Louboutin pumps, or maybe you're thinking of the pair of leather boots you've had your eye on. Whatever pair of shoes you're imagining, these shoes cost a lot of money.

Now, imagine that a friend gets you these shoes for your birthday. You've never received a gift so extravagant, and you promise to take good care of them. Since you know how expensive these shoes were, you store them in their box in your closet. They don't get mixed in with all your other shoes, and you only wear them on special occasions. When you wear them, you're careful not to scuff them, and you even wipe them down after every use. And when a friend asks if she can borrow them, you shake your head. This pair of shoes was only meant for you.

As you clean your closet one day, you pick up a pair of pumps that you had forgotten about. You used to wear them all the time in college. And you remember how excited you were when you got them for less than $20 at Target. They have lots of scuff marks on them, and the heel is almost completely worn off. Since you have your dream pair of shoes, you throw the old, cheap pair in the trash because they aren't even good enough to donate to Goodwill.

When I was upset that men weren't treating me like I wanted, God showed me I was viewing myself and my worth like these cheap pair of pumps. God created me to be treated with care, just like the expensive pair of shoes. But instead of carrying myself like the masterpiece God created me to be, I gave myself away to any decent man who looked my way. I saw myself like the cheap pair of pumps, so the men I dated saw me the same way. I didn't respect myself or my body, so men didn't care if they used me once and then tossed me to the side.

God showed me that in order for men to see my worth, I had to believe how much I was worth to Jesus. After God revealed this shoe metaphor, he whispered to my heart. "You are like a pair of gold pumps, set apart for my glory. Are you going to act like it?"

Once I understood my worth, I walked in confidence in who I was. When men made suggestive remarks, implying that they wanted to hook up, I turned them down. When guys from my past texted me or slid into my DMs on Instagram, I ignored them or told them I wasn't interested. I knew my worth in Jesus Christ, and I no longer needed a man's attention to determine my value.

My friend, you are worth more than you can imagine. Understanding your value sets the foundation for how a man respects and treats you in a relationship.

I want you to close your eyes for a few minutes and ask God to reveal what he says about you. Describe in your own words how much you are worth to God.

When dating or in a relationship, have you been carrying yourself like the cheap pair of pumps, or like your dream pair of shoes? What can you do differently to carry yourself like the gold vessel God created you to be?

When you know your worth, you won't settle or tolerate men that treat you less than you deserve. And when you understand that your worth is defined by Jesus, and not your relationship status, you'll have more confidence as a single woman. Being in a relationship or getting married does not define you.

You are a gold vessel, set apart for God's glory. I pray God brings you a godly man who looks at you how Jesus sees you—chosen and set apart, wonderfully and remarkably made as a daughter of God.

Pray the prayer below, or pray what God is putting on your heart.

God, thank you for choosing me and setting me apart before I was even born. Thank you for sending your son Jesus to die for my life, and for believing that I am worth dying for. Help me see myself like you see me, as a masterpiece and a gold vessel. In Jesus' name, amen.

Surrendering Insecurities

"I will praise you because I have been remarkably and wondrously made."

Psalm 139:14 CSB

I used to think men would find me more attractive and would want to date me if I could change a certain body part. With my appearance overall, I was happy with the body God gave me. But if I was insecure about one body part? It would be my thighs.

I saw other girls around me, and I would envy their skinny thighs. I longed for lean thighs that wouldn't bulge out in a pair of shorts or in a bathing suit. But no matter how much dieting, running, or toning exercises I did, I couldn't change the shape of my thighs.

When I was on the dating apps, I also felt insecure about not having blonde hair. I convinced myself that men found blondes more attractive, and I believed I wasn't as pretty or hot compared to blonde girls. Deep down, I didn't want to dye my hair. I enjoyed being a brunette, and I knew there were guys who thought brunettes were sexy.

Over time, God taught me how to embrace my thighs, curves, and brunette hair instead of desiring a shape and look that I wasn't. But my insecurities held me back from believing that men wanted to date me.

This week is all about learning to love yourself and appreciate who God made you to be. Remember, if you want a guy to love you, it starts with loving yourself. But how do you deal with the things that you don't like about yourself? Today, we're discussing how to surrender our insecurities to God.

Read Judges 6:11-16. God called Gideon a valiant warrior, but Gideon didn't see himself that way. How do you think Gideon viewed himself when God first appeared to him?

Gideon had every right to doubt himself. He was the youngest in his family, and his family was the weakest of their tribe. But God saw Gideon's potential, not his past or even his present troubles. Even though Gideon was insecure and hiding out of fear, God saw him as a valiant warrior.

Gideon wasn't the only warrior in the Bible who felt insecure. Read Exodus 3:11 and 4:10-13 to see how Moses responded when God called him to save the Israelites. What was Moses insecure about? Why do you think he doubted whether God could use him?

Moses felt insecure about his speech, and he was probably feeling shame about his past after murdering an Egyptian. He likely wondered if the men who knew about the murder were still alive, or if they would try to kill him.

It's easy to judge how Gideon and Moses responded to God. How dare they question whether God can use them? It's obvious that

God had chosen both of them to be warriors to save the Israelites, so why was it so hard for them to believe it?

When navigating the dating scene, we can respond the same way to God without even realizing it. We know we are God's masterpiece, chosen and created to be set apart as gold vessels, but we still doubt how a guy would be interested in us.

Maybe you doubt whether any man will love you, or if you'll ever get married. Or maybe you think you're still single because you don't look a certain way, or because you don't possess a certain personality trait. If you've had rocky relationships with men in the past, it's easy to believe what others have spoken over you instead of believing what God says about you. Or if a guy cheated on you, it's easy to believe that you're not good enough.

Over time, these doubts, lies, and insecurities that we believe hold us back from the plans—and future husband—that God has for us.

Dictionary.com[4] defines an insecurity as "a lack of confidence or assurance, or self-doubt." Insecurities are things we believe about ourselves that rob us from having the confidence to be our true selves. If we don't learn to deal with our insecurities, they can prevent us from stepping out into the dating scene at all.

I want you to think of a close friend. Imagine she comes up to you in tears. She just found out that the guy she likes is dating someone else, and she says that she isn't good enough. She calls herself fat, saying she isn't pretty enough, and that no guy will ever like her.

What would you say to her right now? What truths from God's Word would you speak over her to remind her what God says about her?

If you remember the scriptures from day 1 of this week, you would probably tell your friend something like, "Girl, you are not fat. You are beautiful, and God made you unique for a reason. He knows every hair on your head, and you are a masterpiece. If any guy doesn't see this, it's his loss."

Now I want you to imagine that this girl is you. You just found out that the guy you like is dating someone else. Would you still declare these same truths from God's Word over your life? Or would you remind yourself of all your insecurities?

We can be our own worst inner critic. We say things about ourselves that we would never say to a friend. Maybe you reject your thighs like I did, or maybe you put yourself down in other ways. For example, maybe you don't think you're smart enough, funny enough, or outgoing enough. Or maybe you're self-conscious about your chest size, or insecure that your stomach sticks out in certain outfits.

Read Isaiah 45:9-12.

The NLT version of Isaiah 45:10 says, "How terrible it would be if a newborn baby said to its father, 'Why was I born?' or if it said to its mother, 'Why did you make me this way?'"

When we put ourselves down and doubt who God made us to be, we are questioning God's work as our creator and artist. How many times have you wondered, "God, why did you make me this way? Why am I a brunette when I want to be a blonde? Why are my boobs so small? Why are my thighs so big?"

When we carry insecurities around with us, we are essentially telling God that he's made a mistake. And when we reject certain parts about ourselves that we don't like, we are actually rejecting God himself as our creator.

But as the Bible says in Isaiah 64:8, God is our Father. We are the clay, and he is the potter—the ultimate artist. We are formed by the work of his hands.

My friend, God does not make mistakes. He designed you by hand, and he had every detail of you in mind when he created you. And he is well pleased with every hair and bump on your body.

What insecurities about yourself do you need to surrender to God?

What scriptures or truths from God's Word can you declare over these areas? Go back to the scriptures from day 1 of this week if you need a refresher of what God says about you.

Whatever insecurities the Holy Spirit is highlighting right now, it's time to surrender them to God. It's time to declare who God says you are, instead of letting your insecurities hold you back from meeting your future husband.

Pray the prayer below, or pray what God is putting on your heart.

God, I thank you that I am wonderfully and remarkably made. I surrender these insecurities to you, and I ask for your forgiveness for questioning the work of your hands. You made me to be unique, and you do not make mistakes. Help me see the beauty in the areas that I have been rejecting. In Jesus' name, amen.

Insecurities Don't Go Away When You Get Married

I couldn't end this day without sharing about the insecurities I've dealt with in marriage. My friend, if you think finding a husband will fix your insecurities, it doesn't work that way. Insecurities are tough to deal with when you're single, but they won't automatically go away when you get married.

Like many people, I wore sweatpants for months during the pandemic. But when I put on a pair of jeans one day, I realized I had gained weight. Some days, I felt so insecure about my body that I cried on the bed instead of getting dressed for church. I knew my husband thought I was sexy, but I didn't see myself that way in the mirror.

I thought I would feel more beautiful and confident once I got married, but I've still struggled with insecurities. And even though I'm married, I still had to learn how to surrender my insecurities to God.

Insecurities may never go away. But you can learn how to face them now as a single woman.

Comparison: The Confidence Killer

"Pay careful attention to your own work, for then you will get the satisfaction of a job well done, and you won't need to compare yourself to anyone else."

Galatians 6:4 NLT

The more I swiped left and right on the dating apps, the less confident I felt about this whole dating thing. At the time, I lived in Chicago, one of the largest cities in the U.S. I figured I had a good chance of meeting my husband there, but why was it so hard to meet someone? And why wasn't I getting asked out?

After months went by without a date, I felt worse about myself. I didn't feel pretty compared to the skinny blondes I saw around me at the bar. How come guys always went for the same type of girl? And how come my friend met her boyfriend on a dating app, but I haven't met anyone yet?

I was so frustrated one day that I deleted all the dating apps from my phone. I couldn't put up with the virtual rejection anymore. And I was losing confidence in who I was. When my friends talked about all the new guys they were meeting on the apps, I felt jealous. I didn't want to hear about all the cute dates they went on. I was still single on my couch on a Friday night, and it wasn't fair.

What I didn't realize at the time was the root of my low self-esteem and bitterness. The reason I lost my confidence and felt jealous of other women around me? Comparison.

I believed I wasn't good enough compared to the other women around me. Today, we're going to talk about comparison, and what to do when we compare our lives—and our love stories—to others around us.

Read Genesis 29:16-35 and Genesis 30:1-24. Rachel and Leah had something that the other sister wanted. What was each sister jealous of?

Was Rachel or Leah ever satisfied once they started having children?

Rachel and Leah's story is one of the most tragic examples of comparison in the Bible. In the beginning, Leah wanted to feel loved by her husband, Jacob. But Jacob was in love with Leah's sister, Rachel. If anyone had the right to compare themselves, it would be Leah. She's married to the same man as her sister, and doesn't feel loved by her own husband. Eventually, God blesses Leah with babies, but Leah still desires her husband's affection.

How does Rachel feel in the love triangle? In Genesis 29:30, it says that Jacob loved Rachel more than Leah. But instead of focusing on how much her husband loved her (and how much God loved her by providing a husband), Rachel focused on what she didn't have. She could have chosen to be grateful for what God had blessed her with, but she started comparing her family size to Leah's, and she envied her sister.

Their family feud escalates, and the comparison battle gets worse. Back then, if a woman couldn't get pregnant, it was custom for the husband to conceive through his wife's slave. Any children born by the slave would be considered the wife's own children. Since Rachel couldn't get pregnant, she told Jacob to sleep with her slave. Even after her slave conceived, it still wasn't enough. In Genesis 30:7-8, her slave conceived again, and Rachel responds with, "In my wrestlings with God, I have wrestled with my sister and won." (CSB). Having the most babies became a competition, and Rachel and Leah were envious of everything the other sister had.

When you're single, it's easy to compare your relationship status to someone else. It's easy to feel jealous when a friend starts dating someone, or when a friend gets married. Deep down, you know you should be happy for them, but sometimes you can't ignore the feelings of envy and comparison that creep in. You may even ask yourself, "Why does she get a boyfriend and I don't? I've been praying and obeying God, so when will it be my turn?"

If you're struggling with comparison or jealousy, it's important to understand that these emotions are not from God. In James 3:15, the Bible says that bitter envy and selfish ambition are earthly, unspiritual, and demonic. The devil wants you to compare your life to others because it robs you from appreciating the blessings God has already given you. And when you compare yourself to others, comparison brings bitterness and jealousy along with it.

Whether or not you realize it, when you compare, you are questioning whether God has made a mistake in your life. Comparison is essentially saying, "God, why don't I have that? Why did you answer their prayers, but not mine? I thought you were supposed to be a good heavenly Father. Why are you withholding things from me?" If you don't deal with the comparison in your heart, you may even feel bitter against God as you question why he's not answering your prayers.

Yesterday, we talked about dealing with our insecurities. Comparison and insecurities go hand in hand. If we don't deal with our insecurities, we will constantly compare ourselves to other women and think that we aren't enough.

How have you been comparing yourself to others? Do you feel jealous of other couples or women around you?

How can you be happy for others who get married, when you feel left out? I listened to an episode about singleness by Annie F. Downs on the *That Sounds Fun Podcast*[5]. Annie said something that has changed how I handle comparison in all areas of my life. When you feel left out when your friends get married, remember that "no one is getting what God has for you."

If you're submitted to God and obedient to him, you can trust that God will not give your future husband to someone else. When you are jealous of a friend's new boyfriend or fiancé, remember that she did not steal the man who God has picked out for you. You can choose to stay bitter and jealous, or you can choose to surrender these feelings to God. Just like you, your friend has been praying and waiting to meet her future husband, and you can choose to celebrate that God brought them together.

In Matthew 7:7-12, the Bible says that God delights in giving good gifts to his children. If you haven't met your future husband yet, trust that it's for your own good. God's timing and plans are higher than you could ever understand. Instead of focusing on why you don't have a husband yet, shift your focus back to God and thank him for all the blessings he's already given you.

Write all the ways God has been moving in your life and thank God for the prayers he's already answered.

Once you start dating someone, it's also important not to compare your love story to someone else's. You may want to compare your timeline to another couple. For example, you may think something is wrong if your boyfriend hasn't said "I love you" or put a ring on your finger yet. Every God-written love story is different. If you focus on the pieces of your story that don't look like you imagined, it will rob you from enjoying the love story that God is unfolding before you.

If you want to celebrate what God is doing in your friend's lives, and regain your trust in God's plans for your love story, it's time to surrender comparison. And it's time to surrender the jealousy and envy that you've been holding on to.

The first step to dealing with comparison is to repent and surrender it to God. Pray the prayer below to release comparison.

God, I surrender this comparison to you. I repent and surrender any feelings of bitterness or jealousy. Forgive me for comparing my life to others. You know what's best for me, and I trust that you have not made a mistake. In Jesus' name, amen.

Battle Plan to Fight Comparison

Surrendering comparison and bitterness in your heart to God is the first step, but it's important to have a battle plan when comparison creeps up in the future.

In an Instagram-highlight-reel world, we have to learn how to overcome comparison. We're surrounded by photos of people enjoying their best lives, and there will always be someone who has something you want. Instead of letting comparison take over, learn how to celebrate what God is doing for them, and feel grateful for what God is doing in your own life.

When you're tempted to compare your relationship status to someone else, remember the steps below.

1. Let their love story be an example of what God is capable of. If God can do it for them, he can do it for you. Pray and thank God for moving in their life.
2. When a friend gets married, remind yourself that she did not steal the man God has for you. God will not give your future husband to someone else.
3. Remember all the ways God is moving in your life and thank God for all the prayers he has already answered.
4. Thank God in advance for writing your love story and for bringing you and your future husband together.

Using Beauty for God's Glory

"Charm is deceptive and beauty is fleeting, but a woman who fears the Lord will be praised."

Proverbs 31:30 CSB

It was a few months after I decided to stop having sex before marriage, and I finally felt like I was making progress in the right direction. I stopped talking to Jake, and I was learning how to say no to men who didn't have good intentions. But one day as I walked along the boardwalk, I felt convicted. A few men eyed my outfit, and I crossed my arms over my stomach.

I lived in Pacific Beach, which is like the crop top capital of California, so I wore what most women in their twenties wore. High-waisted denim shorts and a fitted crop top. The Holy Spirit spoke to me so clearly in that moment. "I'm proud of you for deciding to pursue purity on the inside, but now it's time to reflect that decision on the outside."

As I looked through my closet that night, my heart sank. Deep down, I felt more attractive when I could show off my body in short dresses and skirts. Besides, everyone wore revealing clothes here, so what was the big deal? For a few weeks, I wrestled with the Holy Spirit. I tried to pretend that it was still okay to wear the same outfits. But after I continued getting attention from the wrong type of men, God made it clear. These outfits were not pleasing to him, and dressing this way would only attract the men I wanted to stay away from.

Today, we'll discuss how to balance beauty with modesty, and how you can honor God with your body as a single woman.

Read 1 Timothy 2:9-10. How would you describe modesty in your own words?

Over the years, modesty has become a controversial topic within the church. Some women cover up as much as possible, and don't wear form-fitting clothing or makeup at all. Other women think that covering up beauty was not God's intent. They feel that they have the right to wear whatever they please, especially since fashion styles have changed since biblical times.

While culture's attire for women has changed, we cannot lose sight of God's definition of beauty, and how he intended for women to use beauty for his glory. In Proverbs 7, the Bible talks about how beauty was not intended for lustful pleasures. In 1 Corinthians 6:20, God calls us to honor our bodies. And in Esther's story, God shows us he can use beauty to win favor from others.

We are called to use beauty for God's glory, but we are not to exploit this beauty. As the Bible talks about in 1 Timothy 2:9-10, we are called to attract attention from others by the things we do for God, not from our appearance.

What's a single woman supposed to do? Does this mean women should cover up or hide their beauty? With dating, it's important to lead with the beauty in your heart and not just your outward beauty. You should make an effort with your appearance on a date, but there's a difference between dressing a certain way to feel confident, and wearing something for the wrong reasons.

Women should not use beauty in a sexual way to attract a man

A man will fall in love with you for your heart, not your body. Like we talked about in week 1, sex does not equal love. If a man claims to be in love with you for your body, he's probably feeling lust toward you—not love. If you rely on beauty or sex appeal to find a man, this will not attract the type of godly man you are looking for.

As I continued on my modesty journey with God, I realized I was super focused on my appearance when I went to church. Since I saw the guy I liked every Sunday, I spent extra time curling my hair and scrutinizing my outfit in the mirror.

Again, I think you should look beautiful and put your best self out there when you're single. But you have to make sure you're wearing something for the right reasons. If I had any doubt about whether an outfit was appropriate, I asked myself, "Am I trying to get a man to see my heart, or am I trying to get a man to notice my body?" The Holy Spirit convicted me several times when I would put on a form-fitting skirt or tight pair of jeans, saying, "Girl, you know you're only wearing that outfit so that guy will notice your butt."

After God convicted me to dress more modestly in person, he then convicted me with my social media. I realized I had been posting photos, hoping to get men to notice my body. You know all those poses where you stand a certain way to get your butt to look bigger? Yeah, God wasn't a fan of all those poses.

As women of God living in an Instagram world, we have the responsibility to be modest in our appearance both in person and on social media. How you dress during the week and how you present yourself on social media are just as important as how you dress at church on Sundays.

Are your social media posts honoring God? Do the outfits you wear during the week reflect the same outfits you would wear to church? Do your outfits and poses look like women from the world? Or can someone tell from your feed that you're a woman set apart for God?

Write what the Holy Spirit reveals about how you dress or what you post online.

If you like to wear revealing outfits or post certain photos on social media, why do you think you present yourself this way? Ask the Holy Spirit to reveal why you like to dress or look a certain way.

After I stopped wearing revealing outfits, I didn't feel as confident about myself. How was I supposed to compete with the other girls that were showing off their bodies? Even at church, I still struggled with the lie that a guy may not be interested in me since I wasn't blonde. But God worked in my heart even more. As I surrendered my doubts to God, he showed me I needed to see myself how he saw me—beautiful—without any heavy makeup or form-fitting outfits.

Women should not rely on beauty alone to feel beautiful

The NLT version of 1 Timothy 2:9-10 says that women should not draw attention to themselves by their hair or clothing, but rather "women who claim to be devoted to God should make themselves attractive by the good things they do." In 1 Samuel 16:7, God emphasizes the importance of our hearts above external appearance. "The Lord doesn't see things the way you see them. People judge by outward appearance, but the Lord looks at the heart." (NLT)

God created women to be beautiful, but we should not rely on our external appearance alone to feel beautiful. It's what in our hearts that make us beautiful. With dating, a man may think you're attractive, but what really captures his heart is when he sees your heart.

When you rely on beauty and hide behind all the makeup, eyelashes, heels, and sexy outfits, it can be hard for a man to see your true heart. And the longer you rely on beauty or outward appearances to feel beautiful, the more insecurities you can have about yourself. Is my hair messed up? Does my butt look good in these jeans? Should I lose another five pounds?

But when you focus on your inward beauty, you have fewer insecurities and more confidence about yourself. You know you are beautiful in Christ. Even when you have a bad hair day or gain weight, you can have peace. Your outward appearance does not define you.

When you get married, your husband is going to see the real you. You will not wake up with your hair and makeup done, fluttering your fake eyelashes at your hubby. Have you ever slept in fake eyelashes? I did, and it was not pretty.

When you're single, practice showing your friends who you really are. Don't be afraid to show your true self and tell others, "This is the real me, and I'm beautiful."

If you feel overweight or not skinny enough, choose to believe that you are beautiful. Resist the urge to compare yourself to women around you. Your weight is just one part about you. Do you know how many other pieces God created when he designed you? Your personality, gifts, talents, your laugh, your brain, your love for others—God has created so many beautiful things about you. And believe that your future husband will love you for who you are.

Are you focusing too much on your external appearance to feel beautiful? Pray and ask God to show you how beautiful you are on the inside, and how to let your inner beauty take the lead.

Pray the prayer below, or pray what God is putting on your heart.

God, thank you for creating me to be beautiful on both the inside and out. Show me how to use beauty in a way that honors you. I pray that my future husband sees me how you see me, and that he will fall in love with my heart. In Jesus' name, amen.

Dealing with Rejection

"You are my servant; I have chosen you; I haven't rejected you."

Isaiah 41:9 CSB

I matched with another guy on a dating app, but he didn't ask me out. I felt like giving up. What was the point of putting myself out there if nobody was asking me on a date?

I threw my phone on the couch and couldn't stop the tears that had started to fall. This whole dating thing and setting myself up for rejection—I couldn't do it anymore. None of the cute guys at work were asking me out, and the guys I matched with on the dating apps didn't want to go out with me either.

Every guy who didn't ask me out was like a reminder that nobody wanted to date me. I couldn't take any more rejection.

I had to put myself out there in order to find a husband, but was God telling me to take a break from dating? How was I supposed to feel confident about myself after so many guys had turned me down?

Today, we're talking about how to handle rejection in dating, and how to surrender feeling rejected to God.

Read Isaiah 41:8-14. Which statement from God speaks to you the most?

God promised to be there for Jacob and the Israelites, and to help them. With dating, do you believe God is with you on this journey? Why or why not?

If you've been praying for a husband and navigating the dating scene long enough, you've probably experienced some type of rejection. Maybe a guy you liked didn't ask you out, or maybe he started dating someone else instead. Or maybe you had a great time on a first date, but the guy wasn't interested in a second date. If you've spent any time on the dating apps, you probably know how it feels to get your hopes up when you match with a guy, only to feel rejected when he doesn't ask you out.

Rejection in dating does not feel good. Not only does it destroy our confidence, but it causes us to love ourselves less than how God sees us. The devil loves rejection because he wants us to believe that we aren't good enough and that nobody wants us. The devil hates marriage and does not want you to get married. He will do anything he can to convince you that nobody wants to date you, so that you give up on finding a husband altogether.

When we face rejection from relationships, we have to learn how to surrender it to God. Rejection hurts, and only God can heal us from the sting of being rejected. When you struggle with rejection in dating, remember these five truths below.

God has not rejected you

No matter how many men have turned you down or rejected you, remember what God says about you in Isaiah 41. When I'm feeling down about myself or rejected, I reread the scriptures in Isaiah 41:8-14, and I replace 'Israel' or 'Jacob' with my name.

God has chosen you—he hasn't rejected you. If you have the desire to get married, you can trust that God has chosen you to become someone's wife. Just because men in the past have rejected you doesn't mean God or your future husband will.

Rejection is part of dating

If you're dating, rejection can hurt. But not every guy you meet or go on a date with is your future husband.

Unless you marry your high school sweetheart, you probably will face rejection from men. But if you want to get married, understand that rejection is part of dating until you meet the man God has for you.

Your future husband will not reject you

Your future husband will want to date and pursue you. He'll know you are the woman and helper that God created for him, and he will be excited to take you on a date.

No matter how many guys have rejected you in relationships, believe that God has someone out there for you, and that your future husband will not reject you.

A rejection can be a blessing

If you really wanted to be with someone, it's hard to see how a rejection or breakup can be a blessing. But the Bible tells us in Isaiah 55:8-9 that God's ways are not our ways. You may not understand why this rejection is a blessing now, but God works all things for good.

Have you ever heard the expression, "a rejection is God's redirection?"

With dating, let every rejection from the wrong guy be a redirection to the man God has for you. Remind yourself that you're not wasting time with someone who isn't the one. Would you want to go out with someone, only to find out that they weren't feeling it from the beginning? Or would you rather them be honest?

When you meet your husband, you'll be glad it didn't work out with other guys you thought you wanted to date.

Rejection is common in dating, but you'll face rejection in other areas of your life, too. When I struggle with rejection, I remind myself that God must have something better for me. I may not understand why something that I wanted didn't work out. But I choose to believe that God's plans are better, and that he knows what he is doing.

If you're worried about getting rejected, remember that God is on this dating journey with you. Just like it says in Isaiah 41:10, you do not need to fear because God is with you. He wants you to meet and date your future husband, and you can trust God to guide you.

A rejection does not mean that there's something wrong with you

When you're rejected, it's easy to think that something is wrong with you. Maybe you think you aren't pretty or good enough to be in a relationship. Or maybe you even feel that nobody will ever love you.

When you believe something is wrong with you, this is when rejection takes root in your heart. If not dealt with, rejection can cause you to have less confidence and low self-esteem. And rejection can prevent you from making secure attachments in future relationships.

If you've been struggling to feel loved and accepted by others, pray and ask the Holy Spirit to reveal any rejection from your past that needs to be dealt with. Sometimes, you may have experienced rejection from your family or friends growing up that can cause a spirit of rejection in your life. Depending on the type of rejection you've faced, you may need to seek inner healing or deliverance to be set free.

If you're taking rejection personally, remember that rejection is part of dating. It's not about you, but about whether the two of you were a good fit. You will not marry every guy you go out with. Instead of wondering what's wrong with you, acknowledge that he wasn't the guy God had for you.

When you feel rejected with dating, what truths or scriptures will you remind yourself? Write them below.

Don't let a few—or a lot—of rejections hold you back from the man God has for you. Remember what God says about you and believe that your future husband will love you like God loves you.

Pray the prayer below, or pray what God is putting on your heart.

God, thank you for not rejecting me. I surrender any feelings of rejection to you. I declare that my future husband will be excited to go out with me, and I don't have to worry or fear getting rejected. In Jesus' name, amen.

WEEK 2 REFLECTION

Finding Love Starts with Loving Yourself

Take some time to reflect and look back at how God spoke to you this past week. Journal your thoughts below, and consider answering the following questions:

- What key takeaways or revelations did you have this week?
- Which scriptures or Bible verses stuck out to you?
- What are you going to do differently moving forward?

WEEK 2 REFLECTION

WEEK 3

In the Waiting

Refuse to Settle

"This vision is for a future time. It describes the end, and it will be fulfilled. If it seems slow in coming, wait patiently, for it will surely take place. It will not be delayed."

Habakkuk 2:3 NLT

A few tears rolled down my cheeks as I stared at the ocean in front of me. I had promised God I would only date guys that had a relationship with him. Too many men had broken my heart, and most of them didn't have God in their lives. But as I trusted God with my future husband, I continued meeting men that weren't interested in God. *God, are there any guys out there that love Jesus? Do godly men even exist?*

As I prayed my frustrations to God, he spoke to my heart. "My daughter, how long would you be willing to wait, knowing that I will bring the man I have for you? Would you be willing to say no to the next five nonbelievers? What about nine? What if the tenth guy I bring you is the one?"

In that moment, I decided I would not settle for anyone less than God's best. I wouldn't settle for dating a nonbeliever just because I wasn't meeting Christian men.

In today's study, we're studying how the devil wants you to settle as you wait for God's promise to be fulfilled. We'll also discuss how to hold on to hope as you wait for God's best. Specifically, we'll study how Abraham settled when he waited for God to give him a son. God changed both Abraham's and Sarah's names from Abram and

Sarai. We will refer to them as Abraham and Sarah throughout this study.

God made a promise with Abraham in Genesis 12:1-4, where God tells Abraham to "Leave your native country, your relatives, and your father's family, and go to the land that I will show you. I will make you into a great nation. I will bless you and make you famous, and you will be a blessing to others." (NLT)

Abraham obeys God, and he sets out with his wife, Sarah, even though he didn't know where he was going. In Genesis 15, some time had passed and Abraham gets weary. God had blessed Abraham with wealth and livestock, but where is this son who God promised?

Read Genesis 15:1-6. How does God remind Abraham of his promise?

Even though God reconfirmed his promise, we see in Genesis 16 that Abraham and Sarah still doubted. Read Genesis 16:1-6. How did Abraham and Sarah make something happen on their own?

So much time had passed since God promised to multiply Abraham that Abraham and Sarah took matters into their own hands. They stopped putting their trust in God. And they convinced themselves that they had to do something in order to fulfill God's promise.

Abraham sleeps with his wife's slave, Hagar, and she gets pregnant. But this was not part of God's original plan.

Read Genesis 17:1-8 and 15-22. What does God say that clarifies that Ishmael wasn't the son who would fulfill the promise?

After waiting to get pregnant for so many years, they had every right to give up on God. In Genesis 17:18, Abraham was so sick of waiting that he pleaded with God to fulfill the promise through Ishmael. "If only Ishmael were acceptable to you!" (CSB). But God confirmed he would fulfill the promise through a son born by Sarah.

In Genesis 21, Sarah finally got pregnant in her old age, and gave birth to Isaac. God eventually fulfilled his promise by bringing Isaac into the world. If their story was a movie, the heavens would open up and Abraham's family would live happily ever after. But this was not the case. Abraham and Sarah had to face the family drama and consequences of choosing to settle. As Isaac grew up, Ishmael mocked him and Abraham sent Ishmael and Hagar away.

With dating, how many times have you responded like Abraham? "God, if only this guy were acceptable to you! Can't you just give me your approval so I can date him and get married?"

When you're single, you may want a boyfriend so badly that you would rather settle than wait for God's best. But when you settle, you have to face the consequences. It may seem like you're happy in the short term when you're dating someone, but you won't be happy in the long run. The temporary high of being in a relationship will wear off, and you'll see this guy for who he really is. And you may experience heartbreak and pain from trying to force the wrong relationship.

With dating, how many times have you been tempted to take matters into your own hands? How did this work out?

Maybe you've dated someone after God told you not to. Or maybe you stayed in the wrong relationship when you knew you should break up. No matter how long you've been single, forcing things to work out doesn't end well. God does not want you to settle. With marriage, believe that God will bring you an Isaac—someone who represents God's best for your life. When you're sick of waiting, trust God to give you the strength not to settle for an Ishmael—someone who isn't God's best.

When you're sick of waiting, are you going to settle for an Ishmael? Or are you willing to wait and trust God for an Isaac?

Only God can reveal if you're settling in a relationship. But if you're wondering if you're settling, pray and consider the following questions:

- Are you entertaining men you know aren't God's best for you?
- Are you trying to force things to happen in your own strength, or are you trusting God's timing?
- Are you dating nonbelievers because you don't think that you'll find a godly man?

- Are you dating someone out of fear that you'll be alone?
- Are you staying in the wrong relationship because it's easier than breaking up and trusting God for someone better?

The devil will do anything to convince you to settle with the wrong guy. He knows how powerful a godly marriage is, and tempting women to settle is one of the devil's oldest strategies in his playbook. As you wait for God to grant the desires of your heart, the devil will try to convince you that God has forgotten about you. The devil will tell you that you'll never get married, or that there aren't enough men out there.

When you're sick of waiting, reject the lies of the devil. Refuse to settle no matter how lonely or discouraged you feel. Don't give in to your ex when he texts you late at night. And don't give in when the guy at the bar wants to go home with you.

When you're tempted to settle, stand strong and remember what God's Word says about you. Just like Abraham, remember God's promises. Remember that God wants you to be equally yoked in your marriage. Trust that God's timing is best, and that he will bring his best into your life.

Every day you refuse to settle brings you one day closer to the man God has for you. When you look back at this season when you're married, you'll be able to say, "God, the wait was worth it."

When I was tempted to date guys that didn't have a relationship with God, I held on to the hope that God would bring the right man into my life. Even though I didn't understand God's timing, I believed that the right guy would be worth the wait. And he was. After meeting several nonbelievers, God brought me a man of God who was more than I ever prayed for and imagined. Now, looking back, my husband doesn't compare to the men I met, and I'm so glad I didn't settle for someone who didn't make God a priority.

If you've been settling or forcing things with dating, it's time to surrender it to God. Write anything you need to surrender.

Pray the prayer below, or pray what God is putting on your heart.

God, I trust that your plans and timing are perfect. Forgive me for trying to take matters into my own hands. Thank you for giving me discernment and strength to wait for your best. I refuse to settle, and I will not force things to happen in my own strength. In Jesus' name, amen.

Giving Up Is Not an Option

"So let's not get tired of doing what is good. At just the right time we will reap a harvest of blessing if we don't give up."

Galatians 6:9 NLT

I brushed the tears from my cheeks as I knelt on my knees to pray. I had already spent hours in prayer, asking God to confirm whether the guy I liked at church was the one. Why did I like this guy for nine months when he wasn't making a move? Why would God give me desires for him if he wasn't my future husband? And why wasn't God moving?

A part of me believed he wasn't the one, and it felt like my heart was breaking. "I can't do this anymore, God." The tears continued to fall as I prayed. "I don't want to like him anymore if he's not my husband. Please take away these desires if he's not the one."

I wanted to give up. My heart was ready to move on, but I couldn't ignore the desires I still had for this guy. I was tempted to tell God that I didn't want to like him anymore. But I continued to pray and asked God to confirm if these desires were from him. The Bible tells us words we speak are powerful, and I didn't want to speak death over my desires if there was still a chance he could be my husband.

Today, we're discussing how to wait and put your trust in God when you're tempted to give up. Specifically, we're going to study what happens when you give up on God, and how to keep believing, even when it doesn't seem like God is moving.

When I feel like giving up, God reminds me of Moses and the Israelites. After God saved the Israelites from the Egyptians, Moses led the Israelites through the wilderness to the Promised Land. But on this journey, the Israelites got a little impatient.

Read Exodus 32:1-8. What did the Israelites do that showed they had given up on God?

Read Exodus 32:9-35. What happened to the Israelites who had turned from God?

It's called the Promised Land for a reason. God promised to bring the Israelites into a land of milk and honey. The Israelites were aware of this promise, and God told them not to make gods for themselves out of gold in Exodus 20:23. But the Israelites gave up on God when things took a little longer than they had expected. When Moses delayed coming down the mountain, the Israelites made their own gods to lead them. As you can see in Exodus 32, it didn't end well for them.

The Israelites who gave up on God didn't make it to the Promised Land. They missed out on God's promise because they gave up. They decided in their hearts they could no longer trust God.

Have you been tempted to give up believing that God has a husband for you?

When you're single and waiting on God for a husband, it's easy to feel discouraged and frustrated. Why haven't I gotten married by now? It's easy to question God when you think you're ready for a relationship, but there is still no ring on your finger or eligible man in sight.

What's a girl to do when you're tempted to give up? How do you keep putting your trust and faith in God when you are waiting for your prayers for marriage to be answered?

When I'm tempted to give up on something I'm believing for, God reminds me of David and Joseph in the Bible. And no, this isn't the same Joseph who was Jesus' earthly father. We're talking about Joseph, son of Jacob, one of Abraham's great-grandchildren.

In 1 Samuel 16, God chose David to become the next King of Israel, but Bible scholars estimate that nearly fifteen years went by before David took the throne. Not only did David have to wait to become king, but he ended up running for his life when King Saul wanted to kill him.

Read Psalm 13. How do you think David felt toward God when he was running for his life?

At this point in Psalm 13, God had anointed David to become king. Yet here he was, running for his life. Can you imagine how easy it would have been for David to question whether God had made a mistake? Or how easily he could have given up on becoming the next king? I wouldn't have blamed David if he gave up when he was hiding out in caves. David cried out to God, asking him how long this would go on for. Have you had similar prayers with God, asking him how long you'll be single?

David put his trust in God, despite the circumstances around him. He cried out to God in his waiting season and surrendered his heart in anguish. David remembered the promise God had made—that he was to become the next King of Israel—and he refused to give up until God fulfilled his promise. King David became the greatest king and leader Israel ever had.

Like David, Joseph had every right to give up on God's promises for his life. In Genesis 37, God implied Joseph would be a leader, since Joseph had two dreams where objects bowed before him. His brothers were so jealous of Joseph that they sold him into slavery. Joseph became an Egyptian man's slave, and spent a few years in jail after being wrongly accused of rape.

Can you imagine the thoughts and conversations Joseph had with God when he was in jail? "Um, God, this is not what I signed up for. I thought you said I would be a leader one day!" I'm sure Joseph had days where he was tempted to accept his fate in prison and give up. But God had a plan. Joseph held on to his dream of becoming a leader until it came to pass. In the end, God used Joseph to lead Egypt and to save his family's lives—the same people who would become the great nation of Israel.

Through David's and Joseph's stories, God not only teaches us the power of remembering his promise, but he also shows us that waiting is part of the process. God never tells us in the Bible that we won't have to wait. Yet somehow, we've built this expectation in our minds that we don't have to wait on God. We live in a fast-paced, Amazon-prime-two-day-shipping world where we expect our hopes and dreams to be fulfilled overnight. But just because things happen instantly on Instagram doesn't mean God works this way.

God can answer our prayers overnight, but he uses seasons of waiting, frustration, and discouragement to build our faith and to prepare us for what's ahead. King David was not ready to become king right after Samuel anointed him. Joseph was not ready to lead Egypt after God gave him those dreams. Rather, their seasons of waiting prepared them to fulfill their calling.

When waiting for a husband, remember who God is, and the promises he's already made to you. God is faithful. He's an all-mighty, all-powerful God who is in control of the Heavens and the Earth. No matter how long you've been waiting for a husband, or how impossible getting married may seem, finding a husband is not too difficult for God.

While God doesn't promise that everyone will get married in the Bible, he promises to grant the desires of our heart when we delight in him (Psalm 37:4). He also promises we will reap what we have sown (Galatians 6:7), and he tells us it is not good for man to be alone (Genesis 2:18). God also promises that we will prosper, and that things will go well for us if we obey him (Deuteronomy 30:9-10). If God has spoken to you personally and showed you that his plans for you include marriage, hold on to this promise no matter what your circumstances look like around you.

What promises has God spoken over your life as it relates to marriage?

When I was tempted to give up on the guy I had liked for nine months, things were about to shift. God was working in this guy's life, and he was going through a big transition at work. Over the next few months, this guy started talking to me more. He asked for my help at church, and he even texted me to say thank you one Sunday. I stared at the text. "God, what is going on? Why is he being so nice all of a sudden?"

A few months later, this guy started talking to me at a Christmas party. He asked me all these deep, personal questions about myself and my family. And he sat by me several times throughout the night. After the party was over, he even walked me to my car. About a week later, we stood next to each other on New Year's Eve at our church's service. A few days later, he took me out on our first date. Jeff and I officially became husband and wife about nine months later.

Can you imagine if I had given up on Jeff—and God—only months before my husband asked me out? If I had given up and started pursuing other guys, I may have missed out on my husband altogether.

My friend, I don't know how long you've been praying and waiting for a spouse, or how tempted you are to give up waiting for a husband. Maybe you've already given up, and doing this Bible study is your last hope that God will hear your prayers. Wherever you find yourself today, I pray God reveals the promises he has for your life, and gives you strength not to give up.

Pray the prayer below, or pray what God is putting on your heart.

God, I choose to believe that you are faithful. I can put my trust in you because you are my God. I refuse to give up on the future husband you have for me. Thank you for giving me strength and hope on the days I'm tempted to give up. In Jesus' name, amen.

The Condition of Your Heart

"Give all your worries and cares to God, for he cares about you."

1 Peter 5:7 NLT

My friend texted me saying she had important news, so we made plans to grab coffee. When she walked into the café, the huge smile on her face and the glare of the diamond on her left hand told me that her boyfriend had proposed. "I'm engaged!" She squealed. I squealed back, but as I gave her a hug, I recognized the familiar feelings of jealousy and bitterness that flooded over my heart.

When will it be my turn, God? When will I be the one to walk down the aisle with a ring on my finger? I wanted to celebrate that God had answered her prayers, but it frustrated me that God still hadn't answered mine.

As my friends got married, being single and trusting God with my future husband felt like I was on a roller coaster. I felt at peace some days, knowing that God was in control and that he would bring me and my husband together. But on other days, bitterness and resentment reared their ugly heads, and I questioned whether God heard my prayers at all.

What are you supposed to do when you feel bitter? How do you cope when you feel resentful toward others or toward God for being single? We've already studied what not to do when waiting on God for a husband. Today, we'll study Hannah's story as an example of how to wait on God.

Read 1 Samuel 1:1-18. How would you have felt if you were Hannah?

Hannah's husband had a second wife, Peninnah, who taunted Hannah for not conceiving children. In 1 Samuel 1:15, Hannah felt so heartbroken that Eli, the priest, thought that Hannah was drunk while she prayed to the Lord. When Eli accused Hannah of being drunk, Hannah was honest and vulnerable in that painful moment. Instead of trying to cover up her tears or hide her pain, she surrendered how she was feeling to God. In 1 Samuel 1:15 CSB, Hannah admits she was "a woman with a broken heart", and that she has "been pouring out my heart before the Lord... praying from the depth of my anguish and resentment."

As you wait on God to answer your prayers for a husband, have you ever felt heartbroken like Hannah? How have you dealt with the pain of being single when others around you are getting married?

When you're single and waiting on God for a spouse, dealing with pain, bitterness, and resentment is not easy. But Hannah shows us how to deal with the pain in our hearts. As you pray and trust God with your desire for marriage, you have to be honest about the condition of your heart. And you have to surrender all of your feelings and emotions to God, no matter how painful it is. God already knows how you're feeling, and he is the only one who can make you feel better. While friends can encourage and pray for you, only God can turn your pain into joy. Only God can turn your heartbreak into hope. And only God can turn your bitterness into gratitude.

When you surrender your sorrows, pain, and frustrations to God, you invite God in to carry these burdens. In 1 Peter 5:7, it says to cast all your anxiety or cares on to God because he cares for you. You were not meant to carry your feelings alone. God wants to be your comforter and place of refuge. He sees every tear, and he feels your heart when it breaks. And when you surrender how you're feeling to God, the Holy Spirit ministers to you.

Have you ever poured your heart out to God and then felt this unexplainable peace after? It may have felt like a weight being lifted off your shoulder, or like you could breathe again. This happens when you surrender all your worries to God.

God is close to the brokenhearted, and those crushed in spirit. He promises to renew your hope when you come to him. If you ignore the pain or refuse to surrender these feelings of bitterness and resentment to God, these feelings will take root in your heart and fester. Just like a weed that starts out small and spreads all over a garden, these feelings will grow deeper and spread all over your heart. Eventually, you will become so bitter that you will avoid going to God at all. You may believe the lie that God doesn't love you, or that he doesn't care about the desires of your heart.

My friend, God cares, and he wants to restore your hope. God does not want you to carry any bitterness or resentment, and he is ready to uproot these feelings from your heart.

Be honest with the condition of your heart and write a letter to God. Acknowledge what you are feeling toward God about being single. Surrender these feelings and invite the Holy Spirit in to minister to your heart.

Pray the prayer below to surrender any pain to God.

God, I surrender my feelings to you. I acknowledge I am feeling [frustrated, bitter, resentful, angry, etc.] and I release this to you. I do not want to carry these feelings anymore. Thank you for giving me peace, and for restoring my hope. Thank you for ministering to my heart. In Jesus' name, amen.

Like Hannah showed us, admitting the true condition of your heart is the first step to letting God heal any pain or bitterness. But what else can you do as you trust God to write your love story?

Read 1 Samuel 1:19-28 to see how the rest of Hannah's story unfolded. What did Hannah and her husband do the next morning after Hannah prayed in the temple? How did God answer her prayers?

Hannah finally got pregnant, and she dedicated her son, Samuel, to grow up in the house of the Lord. In 1 Samuel 2:1-11, Hannah sang her gratitude to the Lord. In 1 Samuel 2:18-21, God blessed Hannah with more children. As God answered her prayers, it's important to understand when Hannah worshipped the Lord. Hannah praised God after she gave birth to Samuel, but Hannah and her husband also worshipped God BEFORE she got pregnant. She worshipped God as she waited for her promise to be fulfilled.

It's easy to praise God after he blesses you with the thing that you've been praying for. But as our heavenly Father, God also wants us to worship him as we wait. When we worship him despite not having received what we're believing for, we're telling God that we still trust him, and that he's still the most important person in our life. Worship shifts the focus from ourselves to God, allowing his peace to wash over our hearts.

When was the last time you worshipped or thanked God for moving in your life? How can you worship him even on those days when you are sick of being single?

Worship Songs as You Wait for Your Future Husband

When my heart hurt from waiting on God, I played worship songs to remind myself that God is faithful.

Listen to one of the worship songs below, or play a worship song that speaks to your heart in this season. Close your eyes and choose to worship God today as you wait for God to answer your prayers for a husband.

- While I Wait by Lincoln Brewster
- Trust In You by Lauren Daigle
- Yes I Will by Vertical Worship
- Faithful Now by Vertical Worship
- Waymaker by Michael W. Smith
- Do It Again by Elevation Worship
- Same God by Elevation Worship

The God Who Sees You

"... Hagar used another name to refer to the Lord, who had spoken to her. She said, 'You are the God who sees me...'"

Genesis 16:13 NLT

I tried not to cry as the waves crashed at my ankles as I walked on the beach. Earlier that morning, I felt excited to talk to the guy I liked at church. Every Sunday morning, I woke up with hope, thinking that maybe this would be the week he would ask me out.

But instead of talking to me at church, my crush didn't even say hi. It was like I didn't exist at all. I couldn't help but feel rejected by both him and God. *God, have you forgotten about me? Do you even hear my prayers?*

At this point on my singleness journey, I had been walking in God's ways and trusting him with my love life. I was serving in church, being faithful where I was at work, yet I wasn't seeing anything shift. If I was doing all the things I was supposed to be doing as a single woman, why wasn't God bringing me my husband? And why were other women around me getting married and finding their spouse?

I knew what God's Word said, and that God hears every prayer. But in that moment, I couldn't help but feel that God had forgotten about me and my desire for marriage.

Today, we return to Abraham's and Sarah's story to take a closer look at Hagar—the one who likely thought that God had forgotten about her.

On day 1 of this week, you read Genesis 16:1-6, where Abraham sleeps with Hagar and she gets pregnant.

If any woman had the right to feel abandoned, it was Hagar. She's a foreign slave from Egypt and gets caught up in a love triangle between God's chosen couple. We don't see Hagar's opinion or thoughts when Sarah suggested Abraham build a family through Hagar. But can you imagine how Hagar felt when Sarah told her to sleep with her husband? Abraham agreed to Sarah's idea, but it didn't look like Hagar had any choice in the matter. As their slave, Hagar became another wife to Abraham and gets pregnant after they sleep together. When Hagar despises Sarah as her mistress, Sarah mistreats Hagar so badly that Hagar runs away.

Put yourself in Hagar's shoes. What would you do if your mistress tells you to sleep with her husband so they can have a family?

When reading this story, it's easy to take Sarah's side and feel bad for Sarah. She's unable to conceive, and when she gives Hagar to Abraham to get pregnant on her behalf, Hagar no longer acts like her slave. But can you imagine how Hagar must have felt through this entire mess? She gets pregnant by a man she didn't choose to marry, and she ends up being mistreated so much by her master that she runs away.

Read Genesis 16:7-16. How do you think Hagar felt when she ran away to the wilderness?

Hagar probably felt abandoned, rejected, and unseen. But God sees her.

God heard Hagar's cry of affliction, and he sent an angel to minister to her. Just like God made Abraham a promise, God makes Hagar a promise to multiply her offspring. Through this encounter, Hagar feels seen. In Genesis 16:13, she says, "You are the God who sees me... Have I truly seen the One who sees me?" (NLT)

Let's take a second to pause and remember what we learned in day 1 this week. Abraham settled when he slept with Hagar to have a family. God confirmed that his promise to multiply Abraham's descendants would not be fulfilled through Ishmael.

Even though Hagar was not God's Plan A for Abraham, Hagar still mattered to God. He still loved her and cared about her enough to make his own promise to her. In Genesis 16:10, God promised to give Hagar more descendants than she can count. The promise to multiply her offspring sounds a little familiar, doesn't it?

In Genesis 16, Hagar gives birth to Ishmael, but that's not the end of the family drama. Continue reading Genesis 21:1-21. How did God make Hagar feel seen again?

After Isaac was born, Sarah got upset when Ishmael mocked Isaac. Abraham sends Hagar and Ishmael away, and Hagar ends up crying in the wilderness yet again.

But God. He still doesn't forget about Hagar. Once again, he sends an angel to minister to her in the wilderness. He reminds her of his promise that he will make Ishmael's descendants into a great nation. Hagar didn't feel seen or loved by the family she worked for, and the husband she was forced to sleep with. But God loved Hagar enough to send two angels after her in a time of great need.

With dating, have you ever felt abandoned, rejected, or unseen like Hagar? Have you ever felt like you weren't God's Plan A, or that you weren't someone else's first choice? Describe any times where you've felt this way.

If you've been praying and asking God for a husband for a while, it's easy to think that God has forgotten about you. But just like Hagar, God sees you.

In Hebrews 13:5, God says, "I will never leave you or abandon you." (CSB). In Joshua 1:9, it says, "Do not be afraid or discouraged, for the Lord your God is with you wherever you go."

God hears your cries, and he has not forgotten about you or your desire for marriage. It's easy to feel discouraged with dating, but God promises to be with you. No matter what you've been through in the past, and no matter what complicated love stories you've been a part of, God sees you and he cares about you.

Maybe you feel heartbroken like Hagar. Or maybe you've gone through a divorce where you feel like God has abandoned you. Maybe you've gotten pregnant where it wasn't your plan to have a baby. Or maybe someone has abused you, either physically or emotionally, and you are wondering whether your life even matters to God.

My friend, God has not abandoned you, and he sees and cares about every detail of your life. I pray you feel his arms around you right now, giving you a hug, reminding you he is with you and that he cares about you. And just like Hagar in the wilderness, I pray you have an encounter with God that reminds you he is there for you no matter what you've been through.

Pray the prayer below, or pray what God is putting on your heart.

God, you are the God who sees me. You have not abandoned me or rejected me. You see my heart and my desire for marriage, and you have not forgotten about me. In Jesus' name, amen.

The Power of Remembering

"Seek the LORD and his strength; seek his face always. Remember the wondrous works he has done, his wonders, and the judgments he has pronounced..."

Psalm 105:4-5 CSB

Before my husband asked me out, I had days when I felt like giving up on liking him. But after I surrendered my frustration to God, I felt an unexplainable peace. I no longer felt like I had to force things to happen, and I was done trying to get Jeff to notice me. Even though I had peace, my heart hurt for letting go of my dream that Jeff could be the one. I had gotten my hopes up for so long, and I didn't know how to move on when I still liked him.

As I wrestled with the pain in my heart, a part of me felt confused and hurt by God. I didn't understand why I had liked Jeff for so long when nothing had happened. And I still didn't understand why God hadn't confirmed the desires on my heart. God knew how much I liked Jeff, so why would he put me through all of this? My trust in God crumbled. Could I really trust God with my future husband when I felt so let down by him?

As we wrap up the week of waiting on God, we're studying how to continue trusting God even when things don't turn out like you had hoped.

Whenever I needed to boost my trust in God, he told me to remember all the miracles he had already performed in the past.

Read the scriptures below. These scriptures describe some of God's greatest miracles in the Bible. Describe the miracle God performed in your own words, and what you learn about God from each verse. I included the scripture for the first verse to get you started.

Proverbs 8:27-29

"I was there when he established the heavens, when he drew the horizon on the oceans. I was there when he set the clouds above, when he established springs deep in the earth. I was there when he set the limits of the seas, so they would not spread beyond their boundaries. And when he marked off the earth's foundations..." (NLT)

Psalm 106:7-10

Joshua 10:13-14

Acts 12:6-11

God controls the raging seas of the ocean so they don't pass over the sand along the seashore. He showed his power and love for the Israelites when he parted the Red Sea, and when he rescued his people from the Egyptians. God continued to fight for his children when the sun stood still in the sky, and when he sent an angel to let Peter out of jail.

In these scriptures, we see God is an all-powerful, loving God. But why is it so hard to believe that God can and will do miracles in our own life?

On day 2 of this week, we talked about how the Israelites gave up on God after Moses delayed coming down the mountain. If you've read the entire story of how God rescued the Israelites from the Egyptians, you were probably shaking your head at how fast the Israelites lost their trust in God. God performed several miracles to save them from the Egyptians, yet after only a few days in the wilderness, the Israelites complained and doubted whether God was really with them. But how could they turn away from God after all that he had done for them?

In Psalm 106:13, the Bible tells us why the Israelites lost faith in God. "They soon forgot his works and would not wait for his counsel." (CSB). In Psalm 106:21, it says, "They forgot God their Savior, who did great things in Egypt..." (CSB). The Israelites despised the pleasant land and did not believe God's promises, and they did not listen to the Lord.

The Israelites stopped trusting God because they forgot the works God had already done. Sometimes, we can get so caught up in what God is not doing in our lives that we forget about what God has already done. We can doubt or believe lies that God has forgotten about us, or that he doesn't have our best interest at heart. If we're not careful, we can forget who God is, and decide to put our trust in someone or something else.

What is the key to continuing to trust God? How can you continue to trust God despite waiting for your prayers to be answered?

Remembering. When you remember what God has done in your life and when you remember who God is, your faith and trust in God will stand, no matter what is happening around you.

Whenever I doubted whether God could bring me a husband, I reminded myself that if God can control the oceans, then he can bring me my husband. I reminded myself of all the prayers that God had already answered in my life. If God answered these prayers, he could answer my prayer for a spouse too.

The same God who created the heavens and the Earth is the same God today. Nothing is too small for God, so why would bringing you a spouse be too difficult for him?

As you wait on God to grant the desires of your heart for marriage, the best way to grow your trust in God is to remember all he has already done. Remember all the prayers God has answered for you personally, or reflect on the miracles God is performing in the lives around you. If you're struggling to see how God is moving, write the miracles God performed in the Bible to remind you of what he is capable of.

How has God been moving in your life? What prayers has he answered and what miracles has he performed?

When you feel discouraged or lose faith that God has a husband for you, come back to this list. The more you remember what God has already done, the more you'll be able to trust that God is writing your love story.

Remembering is one way to build your trust in God, but God gives you another tool to stand strong when you feel like giving up. The Bible.

When I questioned whether God knew what was best for my life, I clung to God's promises in his Word. God's Word became like a life preserver in the ocean for me. When nothing else made sense around me and my prayers weren't being answered, I held on to what God said in the Bible. Even though I didn't understand what God was doing, I continued to pray and declare his Word. The more I declared and prayed scripture, the more faith I had. My trust in God grew, despite not seeing what I had been praying for.

Below are the Bible verses and declarations that I prayed and declared until I believed them. Sometimes, I started out praying in tears, so discouraged that God wasn't moving in my love life. But by the time I finished praying these verses, I was shouting at the top of my lungs and believed that God was moving mountains to bring me and my husband together.

"Seek the Kingdom of God above all else, and live righteously, and he will give you everything you need."

Matthew 6:33 NLT

God will give you everything you need, including a husband.

""For my thoughts are not your thoughts, neither are your ways my ways," declares the Lord. "As the heavens are higher than the earth, so are my ways higher than your ways and my thoughts than your thoughts..."

Isaiah 55:8-9 NIV

Even though you may not know why you're still single, God's plans and timing are perfect. His ways are higher than your ways, and you can't even imagine what God is doing in this season.

"Take delight in the Lord, and he will give you your heart's desires."

Psalm 37:4 NLT

As you surrender your desires to God, trust God to give you his desires for your life and to grant the desires on your heart.

Pray the prayer below, or pray what God is putting on your heart.

God, thank you for all the prayers you've already answered in my life. You are the same God who performed all those miracles back then, and I believe you can bring me and my future husband together. In Jesus' name, amen.

WEEK 3 REFLECTION

In the Waiting

Take some time to reflect and look back at how God spoke to you this past week. Journal your thoughts below, and consider answering the following questions:

- What key takeaways or revelations did you have this week?
- Which scriptures or Bible verses stuck out to you?
- What are you going to do differently moving forward?

WEEK 3 REFLECTION

WEEK 4

Baggage from the Past

Time for Fear to Leave

"For God has not given us a spirit of fear, but one of power, love, and sound judgment."

2 Timothy 1:7 CSB

My heart raced when I saw I had a text from Jeff. The guy who I had liked for almost an entire year was finally texting me. We had been texting for a few days, but Jeff hadn't asked me out yet.

"God, please don't let him play games. If he's not the one, let me know now so I can avoid the heartbreak." I prayed as I took a deep breath and opened the text. Jeff sent a picture of him with his family, hiking by the ocean.

As I responded to his text with a bunch of beach emojis, I couldn't ignore the familiar feeling of fear that caused a pit in my stomach. While I was in awe that Jeff was finally showing an interest in me, I couldn't help but wonder if he was the same as the other guys. I didn't want to get hurt again. And I couldn't take it if another guy ghosted me.

My phone buzzed with another text. "I just found this amazing trail by the ocean. Wanna go hiking with me next weekend?" There it was. The moment I had been praying for and dreaming about for a year.

I sat down on the couch. *Thank you God, thank you.* A part of me felt like I was in shock. I didn't think this moment was going to happen for the longest time. But this was real. Jeff had just asked me out.

As I thought of a cute and casual reply, another wave of fear washed over me. I forced myself to take deep breaths. Jeff was different. He was a man after God's own heart. All the other men I had dated were men after my body. Even though Jeff had done nothing to make me question his intentions, I couldn't shake the anxiety that plagued my thoughts. The fact Jeff was different seemed to make my heart race even more. He had been a Christian for years, but I had only been all in for God for about a year. I had never pursued a relationship in a godly way, so how would I know what to do? And would Jeff judge me for my sexual past?

This week is all about identifying baggage from your past so you can deal with it before you get married. Merging your life with someone is hard enough in marriage. Imagine sharing a closet, your bathroom, and all your food with a man. If you don't get rid of the baggage from your past, it will only cause more drama and trauma as a newlywed. If you don't deal with it at all, it may even prevent you from meeting the man God has for you.

Today, we're studying how to let go of fear. We'll study Rahab's story from the book of Joshua, because Rahab had a lot of baggage she needed to deal with when she trusted God with her love story.

For context, the Israelites spent forty years in the wilderness. Jericho was the first city they came to after entering the Promised Land, where Rahab lived as a prostitute.

Read Joshua 2:1-24. How do you think Rahab felt when she hid the spies and lied to the king?

Rahab is one of my favorite people in the Bible. After reading these scriptures, I'm sure you can see why I like her. She was bold, she put her faith in God, and she wasn't afraid to stand up for herself and her family. And yes, she was a prostitute, but we'll talk more about that later.

For now, I want you to imagine how scared Rahab was when she hid the spies. Not only did she have to muster up enough courage to ask the spies to spare her and her family, but she also lied to the men that the king sent to her house.

If the king sent men to my house, I would be pretty scared. Can you imagine what the king would have done if he found out she was lying? They would have likely thrown her into prison, or even killed her for disrespecting the king. But Rahab trusted God and did the right thing, despite her fears. She believed in God so much that she risked her own life.

With relationships, fear can hold people back from dating or getting married at all. Some people have a fear of commitment, or are afraid of getting hurt again. Maybe your parents got divorced, or maybe you got divorced yourself, and you have a fear that it will happen again. Or maybe you've gotten your heart broken so many times that fear is stopping you from dating.

If you're afraid to date or get married, this is not from God. The devil loves fear, and he uses fear to prevent us from receiving the blessings that God has for us.

Each one of us has different fears with dating and relationships. The first step to dealing with fear is identifying what you're actually afraid of.

Circle any fears you have below. Ask God to reveal other fears you have that are holding you back from dating.

Fear of getting hurt again

Fear of getting divorced

Fear that nobody will love me

Fear that I'll be single forever

Fear of being judged for my past

Fear of men in general

Fear of rejection

Other (describe it):

Did you know God says "do not be afraid" or "do not fear" about 365 times in the Bible? Do you think it's a coincidence that there are 365 days in a year? It's almost like God knew we would need a reminder not to be afraid every single day.

God knew we would feel afraid, but he doesn't want fear holding us back from experiencing the life he has for us. In 2 Timothy 1:7 CSB, God reminds us he has "not given us a spirit of fear, but one of power, love, and sound judgment."

God is bigger than any fear you face. With your love life, God wants to protect your heart. When I was worried that I would get hurt again, God gave me a vision of him holding my heart in his hands. God told me I didn't have to worry or fear that I would get my heart broken. I didn't have to fear that I would get rejected, or that Jeff wasn't a good guy. This relationship was different. For the first time, I had God with me. And that was more than enough.

I want you to be honest. Do you trust God with your heart?

Now, I want you to imagine that God is holding your heart in his hands. He knows dating and relationships are hard. He knows that in order to find romantic love, you expose the vulnerable parts about who you are. God does not want you to get hurt. When you pray and listen to his counsel, he will guide and direct you on this dating journey. He wants to protect you, and he will show you the man who will treasure your heart.

Don't let fear from past experiences hold you back from the relationship that God has for you. Step out and take a chance, even when you feel afraid. When you step out to date, God will be there every step of the way, guiding you and watching over you.

So how do you deal with fear? Once you've acknowledged the fears you have about dating and marriage, how do you get rid of it?

In Ephesians 6:17, the Bible says that God's Word is the sword of the Spirit. When you pray and declare God's Word, you fight against the devil—along with any fear that is trying to control your life. You have the authority of Christ inside of you, so the devil—and all his spirits like fear—must obey the name of Jesus.

Pray and declare the scriptures below when you feel fear.

"'For I know the plans I have for you,' declares the Lord, 'plans to prosper you and not to harm you, plans to give you hope and a future.'"

Jeremiah 29:11 NIV

"Because you have made the Lord—my refuge, the Most High—your dwelling place, no harm will come to you; no plague will come near your tent. For he will give his angels orders concerning you, to protect you in all your ways."

Psalm 91:9-11 CSB

***"She is clothed with strength and dignity,
and she laughs without fear of the future."***

Proverbs 31:25 NLT

"Haven't I commanded you: be strong and courageous? Do not be afraid or discouraged, for the Lord your God is with you wherever you go."

Joshua 1:9 CSB

Now that you know what God's Word says about fear, it's time to surrender these fears to God. It's time to walk in the freedom that Jesus Christ already died to give you.

Pray the prayer below, or pray what God is putting on your heart.

God, thank you for not giving me a spirit of fear, but a spirit of love, power, and a sound mind. I surrender all my fears about dating and marriage to you. I command any spirit of fear to leave in Jesus' name. I put my trust in you, and I will not let fear hold me back from the husband you have for me. In Jesus' name, amen.

Forgiven & Redeemed

"'I—yes, I alone—will blot out your sins for my own sake and will never think of them again.'"

Isaiah 43:25 NLT

I sat in my church's growth class for people who were new to the church. The instructor talked about how God wanted to use each one of us for his glory, but I couldn't ignore the questions that swirled in my mind since I had started the class.

Could God really use someone like me, someone with a dark past, to make a difference? How could God use someone like me for his glory?

Instead of feeling excited about my future, I felt disqualified. I wasn't good enough compared to the "super Christians" around me. I felt like I was tainted goods, and that I wouldn't be as useful to the church. And even though I surrendered sex before marriage to God, I wondered if any Christian guy would want to date me.

As I studied the Bible and learned about my new life in Christ, I stumbled across stories that gave me hope. If God redeemed Rahab's life, and if God used Paul to write most of the New Testament, maybe God could use someone like me.

Today, we continue to study Rahab's story. Specifically, we'll talk about how God redeemed and restored Rahab's past into a life she never could have imagined.

Yesterday, we talked about Rahab's faith and courage to hide the Israelite spies on her roof. Read Joshua 6:20-25 to find out if the

Israelites saved Rahab from destruction.

Joshua and the spies kept their promise, and they spared Rahab and her family from being destroyed with the rest of Jericho. God honored Rahab's faith and saved her, but what happened after that? What did her new life with God look like? We don't know how long Rahab lived as a prostitute in Jericho, but the city that was destroyed may have been the only home she ever knew.

How do you think Rahab felt when she first joined the Israelites?

Put yourself in Rahab's shoes when she first joined the Israelite's camp. Rahab may have still felt the adrenaline rush of being saved from destruction, but she was probably feeling a mix of shame and condemnation from her past. She was a foreigner among God's people who knew she was a prostitute. Her faith in God was new to her. Even among a community of godly people, we can only imagine the looks, stares, and things other women said about Rahab behind her back.

Rahab had a choice to act in faith to save the spies, but the Bible doesn't talk about the other choice that Rahab faced. Would she accept this new life with God, or would she let the guilt and shame from her past hold her back?

Read Matthew 1:1, 2, 5, 16 to see what kind of life Rahab lived. How did God bless Rahab after he saved her from destruction?

These scriptures always give me goosebumps. Not only did God save Rahab and her family, but he blessed her. God gave Salmon to Rahab as a husband and also chose Rahab to become the mother of Boaz. We still study Ruth and Boaz's story more in week 5, but Boaz is known for being a prominent and honorable man of God. In Matthew 1, the Bible tells us that Rahab was part of a very important family tree. She was part of the lineage of Jesus Christ.

Pause for a moment and consider how huge this is. Rahab used to be a prostitute, a foreigner living in a city that God set apart for destruction. She didn't grow up in a community who worshipped God. She didn't attend youth group as a teen, and she did not spend her nights doing Bible studies with other women. But because she put her faith and trust in God, God saved and redeemed her. God gave Rahab an entire new life and chose her to become the wife of Salmon and the mother of Boaz. The Bible doesn't tell us much about their family life, but Rahab must have been a Proverbs 31 wife and woman if she raised a godly son like Boaz. And God chose Rahab to be part of the lineage of Christ.

But that's not all. It gets even better. Read Hebrews 11:30-31. Why do you think Rahab's shoutout in this passage is significant?

As we see in these scriptures, God gave Rahab a special mention in the faith hall of fame. In Hebrews 11, God referenced other notable people in the Bible who also acted in great faith. God remembered Rahab's courage to hide the spies, and she is the only woman cited for her faith in this passage.

Even though we don't see all the details of Rahab's life in the Bible, it's obvious that God blessed her and used her for a specific calling. God redeemed her from a prostitute to a Proverbs 31 woman. But do you think Rahab ever wondered if she was good enough to receive the blessings God had for her?

Rahab's story inspired me as a new Christian. I almost didn't choose to follow Jesus because I didn't want to stop having sex. Once I decided to surrender sex to God, I still continued to stumble. But the fact that God didn't hold Rahab's past against her gave me hope. If God forgave Rahab for being a prostitute and chose her to be part of the lineage of Jesus, maybe God wouldn't hold my past against me, either.

Have you ever disqualified yourself because of your past? Have you ever thought that you don't deserve a man of God?

Compare your life now to your life before you decided to follow Jesus. How has God redeemed your past? How has God blessed you in ways that you never imagined?

My friend, I don't know what type of past you've had, but we've all had some kind of history. We've all fallen short of God's glory. But God's Word says that once we turn to him, he forgives us and remembers our transgressions no more (Hebrews 8:12). He does not deal with us according to our sins deserve (Psalm 103:10-12). Instead, he forgives and redeems us.

If God has forgiven us, why is it so hard to forgive ourselves? Why do we continue to carry the shame and guilt from our past, even after Jesus tells us he does not condemn us?

Rahab could have easily convinced herself that she wasn't worthy enough to receive God's blessings. She could've told herself that no man would ever be interested in her. But she believed she was forgiven, and that God could still use her to do something incredible for his kingdom.

Like Rahab, there were times I doubted whether a man of God would be interested in me. But God brought me a godly man who was better than I ever imagined. I knew I didn't deserve a man like Jeff, but I accepted God's redemption and grace. And thanks to God, my husband and I waited until our wedding night to have sex. God redeemed my love life, and I've been able to share my testimony and love story with women like you. If God can use Rahab's past and my past for his glory, he can use yours, too.

God has already forgiven you for your past, but it's time to forgive yourself. It's time to leave the past in the past so you can pursue the plans—and future husband—that God has for you.

What shame or guilt from your past do you need to surrender to God? Are there any areas you need to forgive yourself, or areas you need to ask God for forgiveness? Write anything that you want to surrender to God.

Pray the prayer below, or pray what God is putting on your heart.

God, thank you for forgiving me, and for not holding my past against me. I choose to believe you are redeeming my past, just like you did for Rahab. I surrender any shame or guilt to you. I will not disqualify myself from the blessings and future husband you have for me. In Jesus' name, amen.

Healed & Restored

"The Lord is close to the brokenhearted and saves those who are crushed in spirit."

Palm 34:18 NIV

I wiped the tears that flooded down my face. I had just found out that the guy I had been casually dating for six months, Jake, was also casually seeing someone else. We were hanging out at his apartment, and I noticed a picture of him and a girl hanging on his bulletin board.

"Who's she?" I asked as I swallowed the lump in my throat. Jake turned to look at the picture. "Oh, she's just a friend." But something didn't feel right. I stared closer at the photo, and noticed that it was a close-up shot, and that Jake was kissing the girl's cheek. The blood drained from my face. After some yelling, Jake finally admitted that he had been hanging out—and sleeping—with both of us.

As I sat on the beach, I didn't care who saw me crying. I knew Jake wasn't ready for a serious relationship, but it felt like a knife had twisted into my heart. How could he do this to me? If he said he cared about me, why would he want to date someone else?

The tears fell harder. Not only was I losing a guy I really liked, but I was losing my only friend in San Diego. God had tried to warn me to end things with Jake a few months prior, but I didn't listen. I thought Jake might change his mind about me and God, and that we would get to be together. And I thought we could just be friends. But I continued to give in to temptation.

I knew God could heal my broken heart, but I didn't know how. How long would it be before the pain went away? And how long would it take to move on and not think about Jake every day?

Today, we're talking about how to let God heal our wounds from the past and how to forgive men that have hurt us.

Read the following Psalms and write each scripture below. I've inserted the first scripture below to give you a head start.

Psalm 30:2

"Lord my God, I cried to you for help, and you healed me." (CSB)

Psalm 34:18

Psalm 56:8

Psalm 147:3

Depending on your past, you may have experienced significant trauma and pain from men. No matter what happened to you, or what was done to you, you don't have to embark on the healing journey alone. The Bible tells us in James 5:16 CSB to "Confess your sins to one another and pray for one another, so that you may be healed."

Talking about the pain with a trusted friend or mentor at church, or a Christian therapist can help you take the next step to letting God heal your heart. But facing the pain from past relationships may be the last thing you want to do. Have you ever heard the expression, "you can't heal what you don't feel?" If you don't open yourself up to talk about the pain, you can't expect to be healed.

God is the ultimate healer, and only God can heal a broken heart. He promises to heal you, but you have to take that first step to invite God into your pain.

No matter how tempted you are to run, numbing the pain does not work. It's tempting to turn to other things like drugs, alcohol, or food. Or maybe you're tempted to busy yourself with work or get into a new relationship. But these things can only make things worse.

Before I had a relationship with God, I thought getting drunk would help me feel better after a breakup. My drunkenness only led to poor decisions, and I felt worse about myself after hooking up with men I didn't even like. The world may try to tell you that the best way to get over someone is to get under someone else. But getting involved with another guy is the worst thing you can do when you're still healing from heartbreak.

Only God can heal a broken heart, and the sooner you surrender your pain to God, the faster you'll be ready for the relationship that God has for you.

What hurt or pain from past relationships do you need to let God heal?

When I was healing from my broken heart with Jake, I stopped seeing him and ended all communication. Even though we stopped hanging out, I couldn't help but feel angry and bitter whenever I thought of him. As I prayed for God to help me move on, he showed me that forgiving Jake for what he had done was a crucial step in the healing process. God told me I couldn't be truly healed until I forgave him.

Forgiveness? Why would I forgive Jake? He didn't deserve to be forgiven after what he did!

God talks about forgiving others in several places in the Bible. In Matthew 6:14, Jesus teaches us how to pray, and says, "If you forgive those who sin against you, your heavenly Father will forgive you. But if you refuse to forgive others, your Father will not forgive your sins." (NLT)

In Ephesians 4:31-32 NLT, Paul urges us to "Get rid of all bitterness, rage, anger, harsh words, and slander, as well as all types of evil behavior. Instead, be kind to each other, tenderhearted, forgiving one another, just as God through Christ has forgiven you."

Forgiveness is important to God, but how are we supposed to forgive those who have hurt us? How are we supposed to forgive the men who have hurt, used, or abused us?

Forgiveness is difficult. Remembering the pain of the past hurts. But if you don't forgive the men or women who have hurt you, God won't forgive your sins. And unforgiveness will become a snare in your life. If left undealt with, unforgiveness turns into bitterness and resentment, and can cause a wound so deep that you may never trust men again.

When I wrestled with anger and bitterness against Jake, God showed me that forgiveness wasn't about the other person—it was about me and my heart. God didn't want me to forgive Jake so Jake could feel better for what he had done. Rather, forgiveness was a gift for me. Forgiveness was choosing to invite God in to heal the pain, and to remove the walls I had built around my heart.

We've been studying Rahab's story this week, and how God transformed her from a prostitute to a Proverbs 31 woman. Think of all the men Rahab had to forgive from her past. We don't know how she ended up as a prostitute. In her culture, sometimes the family would sell a daughter into prostitution for money or status, or the king could have summoned her.

Rahab spared her family from destruction when she could have chosen to just save herself. Do you think she had to forgive any family members that may have played a role in her becoming a prostitute? Do you think it was hard to forgive the looks of judgment and condemnation from others? Rahab also probably had to forgive men who had sexually used and abused her over the years.

What men or people from your past do you need to forgive?

Forgiveness is a process. The first step to forgiving those who have hurt you is acknowledging that you need help to forgive them. If you're not ready to forgive someone, pray and ask God to help you. Trust that God will begin healing your heart, and that he will show you how to forgive this person.

If you're ready to forgive people who have hurt you, pray and release this person to God.

Pray the prayer below, or pray what God is putting on your heart.

God, I surrender the pain from the past to you. Help me forgive those who have hurt me. I surrender my feelings of unforgiveness and resentment to you. I forgive this person for hurting me, and I thank you for healing my heart. In Jesus' name, amen.

Daily Steps to Forgiveness

Forgiveness doesn't always happen instantly. After you've prayed and forgiven someone, follow the steps below to continue to walk in forgiveness:

1. When you think about the pain or person who hurt you, remind yourself that you forgive them.
2. Pray and declare scriptures that remind you that God is healing your heart, and that complete healing is possible.
3. Remind yourself that if Jesus died on the cross and forgave your sins, then you can forgive the person who hurt you.
4. Pray for the person who has hurt you. Over time, you'll notice you feel compassion toward them instead of pain.

Freedom from Sexual Strongholds

"Run from sexual sin! No other sin so clearly affects the body as this one does. For sexual immorality is a sin against your own body."

1 Corinthians 6:18 NLT

My heart raced as I checked Jake's Instagram for any new posts. It had already been a month since we stopped talking after I found out he had been seeing somebody else. Even though Jake broke my heart, I couldn't help but wonder what he had been up to. Was he in a relationship with that girl now? Did he miss me?

I knew creeping on Jake's Instagram was like pouring salt into a wound, and that I needed to stop thinking about him if I wanted to move on. I wanted to get over him, but I couldn't stop thinking about all the good times we had shared. Jake had posted a few more sunset photos at the beach, but so far, no photos with any other girls.

God, why do I miss him so much after what he did to me? I prayed as I closed the Instagram app.

Whenever the Bible talked about wicked people in Proverbs, it reminded me of Jake and what he had done. I knew Jake wasn't my future husband, but a part of me still wanted to be together. Why did I still want to be with Jake? Was I going crazy?

Today, we're talking about how to be free from sexual strongholds from our past, and how to approach sex in a way that honors God.

Read 1 Corinthians 6:9-20. What does 1 Corinthians 6:9-11 say about sexual sin?

Describe in your own words what these scriptures tell you about God's design for sex.

When I first established a personal relationship with God, I was hooking up with Jake. I was used to having casual sex with men, so I didn't think it was a big deal until I had the desire to read the Bible. If you know what the Bible says about sex, you can imagine how shocked I was when I found out that God has a lot to say about sex before marriage.

God shows us in the Bible that he created sex to be enjoyed between a husband and wife in marriage. We see this with Adam and Eve in Genesis 2:22-24. God also emphasizes a husband and wife becoming one through sex in marriage in Ephesians 5:31, 1 Corinthians 7:2-3, and Hebrews 13:4.

But what happens when we have sex outside of marriage? Is it really a big deal and does God care if we obey this command?

In 1 Corinthians 6:15-16 NLT, it says, "Don't you realize that your bodies are actually parts of Christ? Should a man take his body, which is part of Christ, and join it to a prostitute? Never! And don't you realize that if a man joins himself to a prostitute, he becomes one body with her? For the Scriptures say, "The two are united into one.""

God tells us he created sex to bond or unite a husband and wife together. This bond creates intimacy in marriage so that a husband and wife would be joined for life. But as we see in the scriptures above, the bond forms through sex whether or not two people are married. 1 Corinthians 6:15-16 is like a warning for a man not to join himself to a prostitute, or a woman he isn't married to, because he will become one with her.

In the modern dating world, this bond or attachment formed through sex is known as a soul tie. In marriage, soul ties are a beautiful thing. A bond or soul tie helps create sexual intimacy for a husband and wife. But outside of marriage, the soul tie that forms through sex can cause pain and dysfunction in a relationship.

When you become one with someone through sex, or have a soul tie with a guy, you essentially open yourself up to whatever they are dealing with. If a guy struggles with depression, lust, or perversion, you open the door for these things to enter your life. Any time we sin, we open the door for the devil to come into that area of our life. And with sexual sin, the devil likes to bring his friends, lust and perversion, along with him.

After sleeping with men, some women have sexual thoughts they never had before, or have the desire to watch porn. If you slept with someone and have sexual thoughts or dreams, you aren't going crazy. You probably have a soul tie and a spirit of lust or perversion to break off. In week 1, we talked about God's definition of love, and how lust is not from God. If you're experiencing strong sexual desires or urges after having sex, this does not mean that you are in love and that you should stay with someone. Lust is a spirit from the devil that can keep you in bondage. But you can break free with the power of Jesus.

Soul ties can also be a reason it's so hard to move on from someone after you break up. Remember how I knew Jake wasn't a good guy, but I still missed him? It was because of the soul tie. I knew Jake was a bad influence, but because we had a sexual relationship for many months, I felt this strong bond or attachment to him. I didn't want to let him go. And it physically hurt thinking about not having Jake in my life.

With sex, our main reason to wait until marriage should be to honor God out of love and respect. But when you're tempted to sleep with someone, remember that there is nothing casual about sex. A soul tie can form, whether or not you intend for it to happen. Over time, these soul ties hold you back and can prevent you from bonding or attaching to your future husband.

Michael Todd, Pastor of Transformation Church and Author of *Relationship Goals*, has one of the best sermons on soul ties (YouTube, Transformation Church)[6]. I encourage you to listen to the full sermon when you have time, but Michael Todd emphasizes that "there is no condom for your heart."

You know those movies where a couple tries to be just friends, but they end up having sex and develop feelings for each other? This is because there is no condom for your heart. You can typically prevent unplanned pregnancies and STDs with a condom during sex. But you can't prevent a soul tie from attaching yourself to the other person.

Do you have any soul ties with people from your past? Are you experiencing any lust or perversion that you need to break free from?

Do you remember what Rahab did for a living before God chose her to become the mother of Boaz? She was a prostitute—meaning she most likely slept with several men—and probably had several soul ties. As part of her transition to living with the Israelites, God probably healed her body and broke off some of these soul ties from her past.

When I struggled to move on from Jake, I got prayer from women at church to break the soul tie. I also spent time with the Holy Spirit, renouncing and breaking any other ungodly soul ties from my past, including soul ties formed through pornographic experiences. After I broke soul ties, I still had lustful thoughts and dreams, so I prayed to be delivered from a spirit of lust.

Freedom from sexual strongholds like soul ties, lust, and perversion is possible—but it takes commitment and work with the Holy Spirit to walk in freedom.

If you've had sex before marriage, or if God has highlighted soul ties you've formed with other men, it's time to get rid of them. With the power of Jesus, you can renounce and break soul ties. And thanks to Jesus, you can be healed and walk in freedom toward the future God has for you.

Pray the prayer below, or pray what God is putting on your heart.

God, thank you for forgiving me for my sexual past. I surrender any sexual sin to you, Lord. I ask that you purify me and make me clean. I renounce any soul ties from my past, and I break them with the power of Jesus. In Jesus' name, amen.

More Resources on Sexual Sin

Sex is just one area to surrender to God as you trust God with your love story. But it's often the area—and sin—that holds single women back from meeting their future husband.

I could write an entire book on overcoming sexual sin and walking in purity, but this Bible study was not intended to cover all aspects of sexual sin. Like I said before, I almost didn't follow Jesus because I didn't want to stop having sex, but God gave me the strength to overcome my sexual past.

If you've been struggling in this area, you aren't alone. Even Christian women struggle with sexual sin, but most are afraid to admit they need help. Having sex before marriage, watching porn, and masturbation can all affect your ability to walk in purity and be ready for a healthy relationship with your future husband.

If you need help to resist temptation, download my free, 7-day resisting temptation devotional at www.funandholy.com/resisttemptation for prayers and scriptures to pray when you feel tempted.

If you don't understand why it's important to wait until marriage to have sex, I encourage you to study sexual purity after this Bible study. Since my sexual past held me back for so long, I created an online course to help you understand God's design for sex, and how to overcome sexual sin. If you want to walk in freedom in this area, check out www.funandholy.com/pursuingpurity for more resources.

Are you struggling with porn? Even Christian women struggle with porn, but freedom is possible. Check out Covenant Eyes' website at www.covenanteyes.com, a Christian ministry that helps men and women overcome porn.

If you want even more resources on sexual purity, check out my top recommended purity books at www.funandholy.com/blog/puritybooks. When I didn't want to surrender sex to God, these purity books helped me understand why sex before marriage was such a big deal, and gave me hope that freedom was possible.

Who's Controlling Your Love Life?

"If you love me, obey my commandments."

John 14:15 NLT

I closed my eyes as I took a deep breath. I had been googling 'what does God say about sex before marriage'. After reading the Bible and every other Christian blog I could find, I couldn't ignore the pit in my stomach. God was making it clear—having sex before marriage was a big deal and it was a sin.

A few months ago, I didn't care what the Bible said about anything. But things were different now. I wanted to follow God and his ways. I wanted a personal relationship with him, but this whole no-sex-before-marriage thing caught me off guard.

How could I stop having sex when I had been having sex for so long? Who would want to date me if I was waiting until marriage? And since I already had sex, did it even matter?

Deep down, I knew that casual sex wasn't helping my chances of finding a husband. I was sick of feeling used for my body, and I was sick of guys ghosting me after we slept together.

As I sat on the beach, God made it clear. I had a decision to make. I could surrender my entire life to him, including my sex life, or I could continue to pretend like sex before marriage wasn't a big deal. But what would happen if I chose not to obey God's design for sex? Was surrendering the rest of my life to God enough?

Today, we're talking about why it's important to obey God's commands, and what can happen to our relationships if we choose to do things our own way. Remember when we studied God's definition of love in week 1? We talked about how we show love through our actions, by sacrificing our own desires out of love for another person. Today, we're taking a deeper look at what love looks like and how we can show our love for God.

Read John 14:15 and 1 John 5:3. Based on these scriptures, how can we show love for God?

Growing up, you may not have had the best memories of the word 'obedience'. As a kid, you knew you were supposed to obey your parents, but you didn't always feel like it. When your parents told you to eat all your vegetables, or not to eat all the candy from your Easter basket, did you listen to them? As you grew up, you probably realized that your parents weren't trying to be mean with all their rules. They set rules out of love because they wanted to protect you. And whether or not you wanted to, you were supposed to obey them out of love and respect.

If we compare our relationship with God to our earthly parents, we are also supposed to obey God as our heavenly Father out of love and respect for him. He sets rules for us to follow in the Bible for our own good. Don't commit murder. Don't steal. Don't marry a nonbeliever. Only have sex in marriage. God didn't intend for these commands to be a burden. In John 14 and 1 John 5, God tells us that obedience is how we are called to show love for him.

But what happens when we choose to disobey God? What if we aren't motivated by love to obey him, and we want to do things our own way?

When I debated whether I was going to give up sex before marriage to God, I tried convincing myself that it didn't matter. Deep down, I wanted a relationship with God and I loved him, but I convinced myself that it was okay to still hold on to my sex life. Surrendering every other area of my life was good enough, right?

Have you ever showed up to church, and the pastor preached a sermon that talked about exactly what you were going through? This happened to me the next Sunday.

"If you want to follow Jesus, you have to surrender your entire life to him. If you give God 90 percent of your life, but hold on to the other 10 percent, it's not good enough. For every area of your life that you are refusing to give to God, you're essentially giving the devil permission to control that area of your life." Pastor Miles preached from the podium.

My jaw dropped. I had never considered that by choosing to disobey God, I was obeying the devil. I didn't know too much about the devil, but after all the heartbreak and pain I had already experienced with men, I did not want the devil coming near my life.

In the Bible, God talks about disobedience in Ephesians 2:2. "You used to live in sin, just like the rest of the world, obeying the devil—the commander of the powers in the unseen world. He is the spirit at work in the hearts of those who refuse to obey God." (NLT)

After that message, I surrendered my dating and sex life to God. The devil would not control my love life anymore. But as I surrendered this to God, he showed me I still had to face the consequences of my past. Disobeying God for so long came at a cost. All the heartbreak, pain, HPV positive test results, and soul ties could have been avoided if I had followed God's ways.

My friend, obedience isn't always the most exciting thing to talk about, but I have an important question for you. Are you committed to obeying God in all areas of your life, including your love life?

Write any areas of your life that are out of line with God's Word.

If God revealed any areas that aren't pleasing to him, are you ready to surrender these areas? If you're having sex before marriage or dating nonbelievers, are you ready to give this up?

You've learned a lot so far in this Bible study, but you have a decision to make. If you want the life and husband God has for you, do you trust God enough to obey ALL his commands? If your heart is racing or if you're sweating as you read this, you can do this. Even if none of your friends understand your decision to obey God's commands, their opinion doesn't matter. God understands, and we are both cheering you on.

Pray the prayer below to surrender your love life to God.

God, you know what's best for my life. I choose to follow you and obey your commands. Forgive me for going my own way, and for disobeying you. Thank you for forgiving me and for your grace. In Jesus' name, amen.

Obedience Requires Action

Deciding to obey God's commands is only the first step. You can say you want to obey God all you want, but if your actions don't line up with what you say, then you aren't walking in obedience. Imagine that you're in a relationship right now. The guy says he loves you, but he doesn't treat you with respect and he's entertaining other women. Based on his actions, are you going to believe that he loves you? I hope not.

With your relationship with God, you can tell him you love him, but you show your love for him through your actions.

In Hebrews 12:1 NLT, the Bible says, "Let us strip off every weight that slows us down, especially the sin that so easily trips us up. And let us run with endurance the race God has set before us." The NIV translation says, "Let us throw off everything that hinders and the sin that so easily entangles."

Throwing off the sin that is holding you back is how you show your love for God in action. Another word for this in the Bible is repentance, which means to turn away from sin and head in the opposite direction.

When I finally stopped having sex, I thought the hard part was over. But the struggle had just begun. Even though I wanted to stop, I stumbled for months and continued to give in when I was tempted. After months of carrying shame and guilt, God revealed what was holding me back. I had decided to obey God, but I hadn't repented from my old life. Like it talks about in Hebrews 12, I hadn't thrown off the people, friends, and things in my life that were slowing me down. I still got dressed in revealing outfits, went to the bar, had a few drinks, and hung out with Jake. I was still entangled in sexual sin because I hadn't repented.

My friend, if you want God's best for your relationships, it's time to throw off anything that is holding you back. It's time to repent, and take action to remove these people, activities, and things from your life.

Pray and ask the Holy Spirit to reveal things you need to remove from your life. Consider whether God wants you to remove men, friends that are a bad influence, forms of entertainment that stimulate lust, or other activities that aren't pleasing to God. Write anything God reveals below.

Now that God has revealed things from your life that have been holding you back, it's time to take action. Again, you show your love for God by your actions. If you aren't intentional to remove these things from your life, they are going to keep entangling you in sin. They will become a snare for you, and will hinder the plans and future husband God has for you.

How do you remove these things from your life? Pray and ask God for the best course of action. Consider taking the following steps:

- End all forms of communication with men from your past (including unfollowing or blocking them on social media)
- Break up with a guy who God doesn't want you to be with, or move out if you're living together
- Get rid of physical possessions that remind you of your past, including things that aren't honoring to God
- Decide not to go to certain bars or places that led you to sin in the past

Throwing off the things from your past is not easy. But what God has for you doesn't compare to what you're afraid to give up. I pray God gives you strength to throw off what doesn't belong, so that God can make room for his best in your life.

Pray the prayer below, or pray what God is putting on your heart.

God, I surrender my old life to you. I repent and throw off the things that have been holding me back. Thank you for giving me the strength I need to let go of the past. In Jesus' name, amen.

WEEK 4 REFLECTION

Baggage from the Past

Take some time to reflect and look back at how God spoke to you this past week. Journal your thoughts below, and consider answering the following questions:

- What key takeaways or revelations did you have this week?
- Which scriptures or Bible verses stuck out to you?
- What are you going to do differently moving forward?

WEEK 4 REFLECTION

WEEK 5

Single & Faithful

Who Are You Following?

"The godly give good advice to their friends; the wicked lead them astray."

Proverbs 12:26 NLT

It was Friday afternoon and my phone buzzed with a text. A girl I had just met invited me to grab drinks downtown for happy hour. I sighed. I was trying to make friends in San Diego, but I didn't want to rely on drinking to meet people. When I lived in Chicago, I had spent too many years in the happy hour crowd. But it never made me feel happy after all the drinks I consumed.

As I debated saying yes to her invitation, the Holy Spirit asked me a question from within. *Would you rather go back to your old ways just to meet people? Or do you trust that I'll bring the right friends into your life?*

The Holy Spirit was right.

Even though I was desperate to meet new friends, the bar-type of people weren't the friends I needed. I would rather be alone on a Friday night than hang out with people who weren't a good influence. Even though I didn't know how I'd meet new friends, I couldn't go back to drinking out of comfort.

Today, we're talking about how to stay committed to God and his plans for your life. This week is all about being faithful with singleness as you wait to meet your husband. We'll study Ruth's story as an example of how to serve God when you're single.

Read Ruth 1.

Life has not been going so well for Ruth. Her husband died and her mother-in-law, Naomi, tells her to go back to her family. Naomi can't provide any more sons for Ruth to marry. Ruth would have a better chance of finding a husband if she went back.

Ruth's response in Ruth 1:16 tells us how she feels about her situation. Can you imagine how hard it must have been for her to leave behind her family and home? What sticks out to you about Ruth's response?

Ruth's response in these scriptures is one of the more popular verses cited at weddings. While these verses are used to express a loyalty between a husband and wife, Ruth showed her trust and loyalty to God. She would rather travel to a land that she didn't know, then go back to her family and their idols.

Does this sound familiar to you? Last week, we talked about throwing off your old life to follow the plans God has for you. Even though Ruth didn't know what God had in store for her, she knew she couldn't return to her old life.

Ruth put her bold faith in a God she did not grow up with. Her first husband may have taught her about God, but after his death, Naomi probably became Ruth's spiritual mentor who discipled her.

The relationship between a mother-in-law and daughter is known as one of the more difficult relationships to navigate. But Ruth's response to follow Naomi shows that their relationship was special. Ruth not only followed God, but she chose to follow Naomi.

When navigating singleness and dating, it's so important to stay committed to God no matter how hard it gets. And you need women of faith around you to support you.

Starting over in Bethlehem was difficult for Ruth and Naomi, but they had each other to rely on. With the messages the world tells women about dating, it doesn't take much to drift away from God and his ways. But when you have other godly women around you, you'll be more likely to stay committed to God, no matter what trials or temptations you face.

Do your friends bring you closer to God and the plans he has for you? Or do your friends tempt you or influence you to drift from his ways?

When I stayed in on weekends instead of going out to bars, I prayed for months for God to bring me godly friends. I still had friends that lived in other states, but when I felt lonely, these friends told me to drink and sleep with someone to feel better. I followed their advice for so long, but these weren't the type of friends I needed in my new life.

God eventually answered my prayers and brought me to a new church, Awaken Church, in San Diego. I felt awkward attending by myself at first, but women made me feel welcome and invited me to different events. I started attending a women's connect group on Saturday mornings, and I ended up meeting the women who became my closest friends and spiritual mentors. They taught me how to pray out loud, and they rallied around me when I was stumbling in sexual sin. These ladies spoke God's truth with love, and held me accountable as I pursued purity. They encouraged me when I needed it most as a new Christian, and they believed God had a husband for me. And years later, they stood by my side as bridesmaids when I married the man God had for me.

As we grow older, friendships take more time to invest in. Your friends may fluctuate in different seasons, but you'll always need women in your corner who believe in the plans and spouse God has for you.

What godly women in your life can you turn to for support on your dating journey? Do you have a mentor to reach out to for accountability? Write the godly friends and mentors God has brought into your life. Reach out and thank them for being there for you.

You were not created to do life alone. God knows we grow and flourish when we're surrounded by godly community, and when we have wise counsel around us. In Hebrews 10:24-25 NLT, it says, "Let us think of ways to motivate one another to acts of love and good works. And let us not neglect our meeting together, as some people do, but encourage one another, especially now that the day of his return is drawing near."

If you need more godly friends and counsel in your life, don't be afraid to try out a new church, or attend Christian events in your area. What if there's a girl in your city praying for more friends like you?

If you need more godly friends in your life, how can you put yourself out there to meet more people?

Pray the prayer below, or pray what God is putting on your heart.

God, I surrender any ungodly friendships to you. Show me which friends need to be in my life. Thank you for bringing godly women into my life. Show me the women I can turn to for accountability and support as I navigate singleness and dating. In Jesus' name, amen.

Faithful Where You Are

"His master said to him, 'Well done, good and faithful servant! You were faithful over a few things; I will put you in charge of many things. Share your master's joy.'"

Matthew 25:21 CSB

Jeff, the guy I liked for an entire year, had just asked me out. I felt like I was floating. Nothing could wipe the smile from my face. But a few days later, my friend from church, Heather, called me. She felt like God wanted to speak to me through a dream she had.

In Heather's dream, the two of us were sitting on a couch. I was excited and told her about my dream to have Asian babies (Jeff is from Taiwan). But Heather saw a baby sitting on the couch next to me. "Don't you already have a baby?"

I glanced at the baby and paid more attention to it. Before Heather had mentioned it, it was like I had forgotten that the baby was there.

As Heather tells me about the dream, she asked if I knew what the dream meant. "Did you already have a baby before?" I shook my head. The Holy Spirit then revealed what the baby meant. "No, but I think I know what God is trying to tell me."

As I surrendered the dream to God in prayer, the Holy Spirit revealed that the baby in the dream was the book God had called me to write a few months prior. Through Heather's dream, God was basically telling me, "Yes, your dream for a husband and Asian babies will come, but you need to pay more attention to the baby I've already given you. You need to be faithful with what I've called you to in this season."

Heather's dream was like a gentle nudge from God to focus more on writing the book he had called me to write.

Today, we're talking about how to be faithful with what God has called you to as a single woman. We will continue studying Ruth's story to see how she served God faithfully before God brought her a husband.

Read Ruth 2:1-13. How did Ruth first meet Boaz?

Naomi and Ruth got to Bethlehem at the beginning of the barley harvest. Ruth wanted to work in the fields to gather grain for her and her mother-in-law. With everything going on, Ruth could have easily stayed at home, sulking in depression or complaining about how single she was. But instead of letting her circumstances paralyze her, she followed the call God put on her heart to work.

Ruth met Boaz working in his field. Do you think it's a coincidence she arrived at the beginning of the barley harvest, and that she found Boaz's field? We can already see God's hand bringing them together.

Read Ruth 2:14-23. What did Boaz promise to provide Ruth if she worked in his fields?

Ruth instantly won the favor of Boaz, where he promised to provide for her and protect her. Boaz even commented on the fact that Ruth has been loyal to her mother-in-law, and prayed that God will bless her for her faithfulness.

Ruth was faithful to work where God had placed her in a new city. She could have focused on finding a new husband, but she got to work. And she ended up meeting her future spouse at work. We will study the rest of Ruth and Boaz's love story later this week, but Ruth shows us how to be faithful as a single woman.

Why is it important to be faithful to what God has called you to as a single woman? Because faithfulness is a big deal to God.

In Matthew 25, Jesus tells his disciples the parable of the talents. When a servant multiplied what his master had entrusted to him, the master called him a faithful servant. "You were faithful over a few things; I will put you in charge of many things." (Matthew 25:21 CSB).

Jesus emphasized the importance of faithfulness again in Luke 16:10. "If you are faithful in little things, you will be faithful in large ones. But if you are dishonest in little things, you won't be honest with greater responsibilities." (NLT)

When we're faithful with little, God will entrust us with more. As we discussed in week 1, marriage is a responsibility and ministry. If you aren't faithful to what God has already called you to as a single woman, why would God trust you with more?

Being faithful when you're single shows God you're ready to be faithful as a wife.

When you're single, it's easy to wonder what your life will look like as a married woman. And it's easy to think that your season of singleness is wasted. That being single is just a season of waiting, and that your real life will start once you get married. But this is a lie. Your life has already started, and you have purpose as a single woman.

In week 2, do you remember talking about how God made you to be his masterpiece? In Ephesians 2:10, God tells us he created you to be a masterpiece to fulfill the works he created for you to do. Christine Caine, one of my favorite Christian speakers and authors, always says, "You were created on purpose for a purpose."

God has purpose for you as a single woman. He has a specific calling or assignment for you to accomplish in this season.

In 1 Corinthians 7, Paul even argues that singleness is a gift because you can focus more on God than if you were married. If you want to get married, it may be hard to see how singleness is a gift. But Paul has a point. There are things you can do now as a single woman that will be harder to do when you're married with kids.

Perhaps it's taking a new job, traveling on a mission trip, finishing school, or serving on a volunteer team at church. Have you ever considered whether God has an assignment for you to fulfill as a single woman?

Before God called me to write my first book, *One Transforming Love*, he put it on my heart to do a rotation at work. I traveled across the country for six months, instructing new-hire trainings. Through this rotation, God confirmed my passion for teaching and developing others, and I developed my teaching skills to use in women's ministry. Not only had God developed my skills and character through this rotation, but I realized I probably wouldn't have accepted the role if I had been in a relationship since it involved so much travel.

When I was praying for my husband to ask me out, God also revealed my unique purpose and calling to write. If I had been so focused on trying to get Jeff to ask me out, could you imagine what would have happened if I missed God's call to write? Who knows if this Bible study would have been written!

Just like God had a purpose in my singleness, God created you on purpose for a purpose. Your life matters now as a single woman. God has given you gifts, talents, and passion to use for his glory. And when you're faithful with what God has given you in this season, you show God that you're ready for what's ahead.

What has God called you to focus on or steward as a single woman?

When you're waiting to get married, it can be tempting to show God that you're ready to become a wife. It's good to understand the role and responsibility of a wife, but you can't ignore what God has called you to do as a single woman. The calling God has for you when you're single is just as important as your purpose in marriage. This season of singleness matters to God, and he wants you to make the most out of it.

How can you serve God more faithfully with the opportunities he's put in front of you?

Pray the prayer below, or pray what God is putting on your heart.

God, thank you for all the opportunities to serve you as a single woman. Show me what you want me to focus on in this season. Help me see this season as a gift. In Jesus' name, amen.

Speaking Life

"Death and life are in the power of the tongue."

Proverbs 18:21 CSB

I didn't seriously pray to God for my future husband until I was twenty-nine. At this point, I had dated a certain type of man for so long, and I believed things about men that weren't true.

For example, since I had terrible experiences with men who were younger than me, I vowed I would never date a younger man. They were immature, and it would never work out. I also believed that there weren't enough Christian men out there. And that men would only want to date me to have sex. After getting hurt so many times, I even believed that all men cheated.

Since my experiences with men had been so awful, I believed all men would act the same way. But no matter how much these beliefs appeared to be true in my dating life, God showed me I was cursing my love life by coming into agreement with these statements.

God showed me that the more I believed and said these statements out loud, the more these beliefs would become my reality.

Today, we're discussing how inner vows or limiting beliefs can hold you back from meeting the man God has for you.

Read Mark 11:12-14.

These scriptures seem harsh at first. Why would Jesus curse a poor little fig tree to die? But as we see in Mark 11:20-26, Jesus was trying to prove a point to his disciples.

Read Mark 11:20-26. What lesson was Jesus trying to teach his disciples?

Jesus taught the disciples that our words have power. If we believe in our heart that God can do something, he will do it. Jesus cursed the fig tree with his words, and the fig tree withered up and died the next morning.

God emphasizes the power of our words again in Proverbs 18:21 CSB, where it says, "Death and life are in the power of the tongue." With our words, we can either speak life, or we can speak death by cursing things around us.

In James 3:2-12, God tells us the words we speak from our tongue seem small, but our words are like a tiny spark that can set a great forest on fire. We can either praise God, or we can curse what God has created. Blessing and cursing come pouring out of the same mouth.

In these examples, God shows us the words we speak have the power to direct the destination of our lives. With singleness and dating, the words we speak have the power to direct our love life.

You may curse your love life without even realizing it. When you make statements that include "I'll never date..." or "I'll only marry...", these statements are inner vows or limiting beliefs. And these types of statements could hold you back from meeting your future husband. For example, maybe you say that you'll only date a guy who is at least six feet tall, or that you'll never date someone who has kids. Unless God has revealed these things about your future husband, these are limiting beliefs that aren't in line with God's will for your life. It's okay to have preferences of what you want in a man, but it's important to make sure you're open to the spouse God has for you. You may think you know what you want, but God knows what you need.

When I said I would never date a younger man, I believed this to be true. I didn't consider dating a younger guy for the longest time. But this was an inner vow and a false belief that wasn't from God. God showed me I had to renounce and come out of agreement with this inner vow. Guess how old my husband is? He's almost three years younger than me. But I may not have considered him if I held on to that false belief.

My husband also believed a lie about what his future wife would look like. He was convinced his future wife was blonde. He admitted he didn't consider dating me when we first met because I was a brunette. No wonder I waited an entire year for him to ask me out. God had to wake my husband up and show him he had been idolizing women with blonde hair.

Looking back at Ruth's story, what lies about herself do you think she was tempted to believe? She was a foreign widow in a new city. We can only imagine the words and labels the community spoke about her. Ruth could have disqualified herself by thinking Boaz was too good for her, or that no guy would want to date a woman like her. Or maybe she was tempted to believe that she would never get married again.

What words are you speaking over yourself and the men around you? Are you blessing your singleness and dating life? Or are you cursing it? As a single woman, there are so many lies or inner vows that you could make without even realizing it.

Circle any of the inner vows or lies you've been believing.

Nobody wants to date me

I'll always be single

It's too late for me to get married

I'll never date a guy who's been divorced, or who already has kids

I'll never date a guy who has a certain skin color, or from a certain ethnicity

I'll only date a guy who makes a certain amount of money

I'll only date a guy who is at least six feet tall

Men aren't waiting until marriage to have sex

All men cheat

We've talked about a lot of topics so far in this Bible study. I want you to write any other lies or inner vows that you've believed that don't line up with God's truth. For example, maybe you believed that you have to have sex with a guy in order for him to love you. Or maybe you believed God has forgotten about you, or that you don't deserve a godly man.

Which inner vows have you believed? For every inner vow or limiting belief, write a scripture or Bible verse that illustrates God's truth in that area.

Inner Vow or Lie	**God's Truth**

It's time to surrender any lies, inner vows, or limiting beliefs to God. Don't let a false mindset stop you from meeting the man God has for you.

With the power of the Holy Spirit, you are going to break the lies that you've believed. Whenever you make an inner vow or come into agreement with something that's not from God, it's important to do the following:

- Repent for believing something that was not in line with God's Word
- Break the inner vow or lie by renouncing it and coming out of agreement with it
- Declare God's truth over that area

Pray the prayer below to break off inner vows or limiting beliefs.

God, thank you for revealing the lies and ungodly beliefs I believed to be true. I repent for agreeing with these lies. I ask for your forgiveness through Jesus Christ.

Right now, I renounce the lie that [say each lie you wrote] and I declare that [say God's truth for that lie].

I break the agreement I've had with this lie or ungodly belief and I declare I have been forgiven with the blood of Jesus Christ. Lord, I ask that you renew my mind and fill me with your truth. In Jesus' name, amen.

Characteristics of a Man of God

"Yes, just as you can identify a tree by its fruit, so you can identify people by their actions."

Matthew 7:20 NLT

When I surrendered my love life to God, I doubted whether I would find a decent guy who loved Jesus. I had a lot of experience with worldly men and had seen several examples of how I didn't want to be treated in a relationship. But I had no idea what a godly man looked like.

Do godly men exist in today's culture? Are there guys who love God and still know how to have fun? And are Christian men really waiting until marriage to have sex again?

Once I started attending my church in San Diego, I met several single men who loved God. But I still doubted whether they were genuine Christians. My friends shared stories of how they dated men from church in the past, but then they realized the men didn't have a deep relationship with God. They thought they could trust their boyfriends since they met in church, but the guys brought a lot of pain and drama into the relationship.

My friends who used dating apps shared horror stories of the "Christian" men they met online. Men said they were Christian, but then asked my friends to see dirty pics, or tried to sleep with them on the first date.

I prayed as I surrendered my doubts and fears to God. "God, I don't want to get hurt by men again. Show me what a loving man of God looks like and show me the godly man you have for me."

Today, we're discussing how to discern whether someone is a man of God, and characteristics to look for in a guy. We continue to study Ruth and Boaz's relationship. Specifically, the characteristics that made Boaz a godly man and honorable husband.

Read Ruth 3:8-14 and Ruth 4:1-10. How did Boaz show he was a man of God through his actions?

On day 2, we studied how Ruth and Boaz met in Boaz's field. Go back and read Ruth 2:8-17. What qualities or characteristics do we learn about Boaz?

Oh Boaz. Sigh. Every woman wants a Boaz, a man after God's own heart, and a man of integrity. But what does a man of God look like? And how do you know when you meet a genuine man of God?

Boaz shows he's a man of God through his actions. From the moment Boaz meets Ruth, he treats her with kindness and respect. He provides food for her and her mother-in-law. He made his intentions clear and instructs Ruth to stay in his field so men wouldn't take advantage of her. Not only did Boaz protect and provide for a woman he barely knew, but he honors her and respects her. Boaz could have judged Ruth or treated her differently because she was a foreigner, but he proclaims a blessing over her.

When Ruth shows up at Boaz's feet on the threshing floor, Boaz covers her so she wouldn't ruin her reputation. He also acted with integrity when he gave the other family member a chance to redeem Ruth and the property. Boaz shows us his character through these interactions, but we see his true heart for God when he becomes the family redeemer.

What does Boaz choose to do when he becomes the family redeemer?

Boaz essentially gave up part of his inheritance when he agreed to marry Ruth. This was custom back then, so Ruth's husband's name could continue to live on. Do you remember how God defines love in week 1? God showed us love through sacrificing Jesus on the cross. And Boaz showed his love for Ruth by sacrificing himself as the family redeemer.

We also talked about showing love through our actions, and not just through our words. God illustrates this concept again in Matthew 7:15-20. Jesus teaches his disciples how to identify a false prophet that comes disguised a harmless sheep. "You can identify them by their fruit, that is, by the way they act... A good tree produces good fruit, and a bad tree produces bad fruit. A good tree can't produce bad fruit, and a bad tree can't produce good fruit... Yes, just as you can identify a tree by its fruit, so you can identify people by their actions." (Matthew 7:16-18, 20 NLT)

What's the key to discerning whether a man is a genuine man of God? Just like you can identify a tree by its fruit, you can identify a man of God by his actions.

A man of God will produce godly fruit in his life, and his actions will show that he is walking in God's ways. You should be able to tell he has a personal relationship with Jesus Christ from how he lives his life. If a guy says he's a Christian, but doesn't act like it, then he probably doesn't spend much time with God.

What does a man of God look like to you? List out qualities that you're looking for in a godly husband, or specific actions that a godly man should do in a relationship.

When I waited for my husband, Jeff, to ask me out, we served on the same volunteer team at church. Through serving, I saw his love for God and others in action. Jeff led his team with confidence, and he always had a smile on his face when he welcomed new people to church. But the thing that stood out to me? Hearing him pray in the team huddle. Jeff's prayers were the sexiest and most beautiful thing I had ever heard.

You can tell a lot about a man by how he prays. A praying man is a sexy man. There's nothing like witnessing a man praying with confidence and passion for the Lord. If you're not sure how you feel about a guy, ask him to pray. You should be able to see a man's love for God and for others when he prays.

If you've been wondering if there are godly men like Boaz out there, the answer is yes. There are men walking in God's ways, including waiting until marriage to have sex. We'll talk more about where to find single, godly men next week, but it's important to know the qualities to look for in a man.

As you pray for a godly husband, it's also important to understand that your husband will not be perfect. It's easy to have the expectation in your mind that if a guy's a man of God, that he won't have any flaws.

But I don't care how in love with Jesus a guy is. At some point in your relationship, he will fall short. For example, maybe he's late picking you up, or maybe he forgot to ask you about that big meeting you had at work. Or maybe he doesn't know how to communicate his feelings as well as you do.

Only Jesus was perfect. While the Holy Spirit is constantly at work in us, transforming us to be more like Christ, none of us is perfect. As you pray for a godly husband, you can pray he has a heart to grow with the Holy Spirit. But he won't be perfect.

Pray the prayer below, or pray what God is putting on your heart.

God, thank you for showing me what a man of God looks like. I pray you are transforming my future husband into a man after your own heart. In Jesus' name, amen.

It's Time to Fight

"A final word: Be strong in the Lord and in his mighty power. Put on all of God's armor so that you will be able to stand firm against all strategies of the devil."

Ephesians 6:10-11 NLT

I was walking on the beach boardwalk when I ran into Jake, the guy who had broken my heart. This was the moment I had been dreading for months. As my heart raced, I remembered to breathe. It had been six months since we had spoken, and I didn't have feelings for him anymore. As Jake walked toward me, I reminded myself that I had already forgiven him. We didn't have to talk about the past.

We shared what we had been up to at the beach and then went on our way. I felt peace knowing that I didn't have feelings for him anymore, but I wasn't expecting him to text me afterward. "It was really nice seeing you. Don't be a stranger now." He even had the nerve to include a wink emoji face.

"God, what is going on? Why did I run into Jake and get asked out by two other guys on the beach?" Earlier that week, two men had approached me on separate occasions and asked for my phone number. I mentioned I only dated guys who loved God, and they both admitted that God wasn't their thing.

No one had asked me out in months, so the timing of all this felt off. Where did these random guys come from? And was running into Jake a coincidence?

As I processed how to respond to Jake's text, the Holy Spirit told me to remember what date it was. I opened up the calendar app on my phone and felt a strong knowing in my Spirit. It was the week before Valentine's Day—of course, the devil would try to tempt me this week. Valentine's Day had been my least favorite holiday for years. Even though I had God in my life, it was like the devil knew I felt lonely this time of year. Running into Jake wasn't a coincidence—it was a temptation. I knew what the devil was trying to do, but I wouldn't fall for it.

Today, we're talking about how to stand strong when faced with temptation, and how the devil will try to prevent you from meeting your future husband.

In John 10:10, the Bible tells us that the thief, also known as the devil, has come to steal, kill, and destroy. In 1 Peter 5:8, it says, "Stay alert! Watch out for your great enemy, the devil. He prowls around like a roaring lion, looking for someone to devour." (NLT)

Since you are God's daughter, created in the image of God, the devil will do anything to destroy your life. The purpose of today's study is not to scare or discourage you, but to prepare you. We know we have a God who loves us and protects us, but there's a devil out there who wants to destroy us.

In week 1, we discussed how marriage is a beautiful covenant God created for a husband and wife. The devil will do anything he can to prevent godly marriages from happening. Since marriage is a representation of how Christ loves the church, the devil hates marriage. And the devil does not want you to get married.

While God wants to bring you and your future husband together, the devil wants to stop it from happening. If you've been facing trials, obstacles, and temptation as a single woman, do not be surprised. This is known as spiritual warfare. Armies fighting military warfare in real life don't play nice. Just like an army will attack an opponent when they're weak, the devil will attack you when you are most vulnerable and exposed.

For example, the devil may tempt you to settle for someone who isn't God's best when you're lonely. Maybe he will convince you it's okay to date a nonbeliever. Or maybe he'll convince you to stay with someone even when God tells you they aren't the one.

The devil may also try to tempt you into sin, bringing destruction into your life and separating you from God. Temptation is a common strategy and tactic the devil uses to get you to sin. He even tried to tempt Jesus. For single ladies, the devil loves using sexual temptation. For example, the devil may whisper in your ear that it's okay to sleep with someone, or that it's okay to entertain an ex because you've been single for so long.

If the devil can't tempt you to sin, he will try to get you to believe lies that contradict God's Word. Remember the inner vows and limiting beliefs we talked about on day 3 this week? The devil wants you to believe these lies. When you believe lies instead of God's truth, you'll stop pursuing what God has for you. Even your future husband.

The devil's ultimate goal is to get you to turn away from God and to stop believing in God's truth. Even the devil knows the power of faith, so he'll try to get you to question who God is and his character. When you turn from God himself and stop having faith, you are an easy target for the devil to destroy.

What spiritual warfare have you faced as a single woman? How has the devil tempted you to sin or tried to get you to stop believing God's truth?

Now, let me reiterate the purpose of this day is not to discourage you or freak you out, but to prepare you. There is a devil who wants to destroy your life, but God had a plan to overcome the devil's schemes. Jesus died on the cross not only for our sins, but to defeat the power of the enemy.

In Luke 10:19 NLT, Jesus says, "Look, I have given you authority over all the power of the devil, and you can walk among snakes and scorpions and crush them. Nothing will injure you." When you accept Jesus as your Lord and Savior, he gives you authority over the devil. This means that the devil and his evil spirits must obey what you tell them to do when you use Jesus' name.

God has given you power, authority, and tools to fight back—but do you know how to use them? How can you stop the devil from messing with your love life?

Read Ephesians 6:10-18. Describe in your own words how you can fight back against the devil using the pieces of God's armor.

Whenever I feel like I'm under spiritual attack, the Holy Spirit reminds me I have authority over the devil, and to use the armor of God to fight back.

Think of the battle you're facing in your life right now. Imagine you are wearing the armor of God described in Ephesians 6. You have the helmet of salvation on your head, and you're able to tie up your sandals with peace because you know God's got you. The breastplate of righteousness covers your chest, because no matter how many times the devil tries to bring up your past, you know you've been forgiven and redeemed through Jesus Christ. Next, you pick up the shield of faith, ready to hold it up against any lies the devil tries to throw at you. When you have faith in who God is, and believe his Word, you'll be able to extinguish the fiery arrows and lies from the devil. As you hold the shield of faith in one hand, you pick up the sword of the Spirit—the Word of God—and you fight back. You pray and declare scriptures over your situation, and you remind the devil what God says. And you tell the devil to back off, and that he has already been defeated in Jesus' name.

How did that feel? Can you feel God's presence or his power inside of you? You are a warrior—and it's time to fight back.

Declare and pray God's Word ("the sword of the Spirit")

Declaring God's Word out loud is the most powerful weapon God has given you to fight the devil. In Ephesians 6:17 NLT, the Bible says, "... to take the sword of the Spirit, which is the word of God." In Hebrews 4:12 NLT, the Bible says, "For the word of God is alive and powerful. It is sharper than the sharpest two-edged sword."

There is power in God's Word, and declaring scripture against the lies of the devil will destroy him. Even Jesus fought back against the devil by declaring God's truth. In Matthew 4, the devil tried to tempt Jesus in the wilderness by distorting God's Word. But Jesus fought back with the correct application of God's Word and the devil left him. This is why it's so important to know what the Bible says, because the devil will try to use God's truth out of context to get you to sin.

When fighting back with God's Word, declare scriptures that assert your authority over the devil. Pray and declare the scriptures below out loud when you need to tell the devil to leave you alone.

"No weapon formed against you shall prosper..."

Isaiah 54:17 NKJV

"So humble yourselves before God. Resist the devil, and he will flee from you."

James 4:7 NLT

""Get out of here, Satan," Jesus told him."

Matthew 4:10 NLT

When facing temptation or a lie from the devil, pray scriptures that declare God's truth over a particular situation.

For example, if you're struggling with sexual temptation, declare the scriptures discussed in week 4 that talk about why it's important to wait until marriage. Or pray a scripture like Psalm 51:10 to give you strength to walk away.

"Create in me a pure heart, O God, and renew a steadfast spirit within me."

Psalm 51:10 NIV

Ephesians 6:16 NLT points out another strategy of the devil. "Hold up the shield of faith to stop the fiery arrows of the devil." You know those lies about yourself the devil tries to get you to believe? Those lies are like fiery arrows.

If the devil tries to get you to believe lies that contradict God's Word, hold up your shield of faith and declare a scripture that reaffirms God's truth. For example, if the devil calls you ugly and says that nobody wants to date you, declare Psalm 139:14 CSB to remind yourself and the devil that you are wonderfully and remarkably made.

In Ephesians 6:18 NLT, it says, "Pray in the Spirit at all times and on every occasion." No matter what the devil throws at you, do not underestimate the power of praying and declaring God's Word, especially when faced with temptation.

God has given you authority and power to fight the devil. He also gives you discernment through the Holy Spirit to discern whether something is from God. Ever heard the expression, "when God wants to bless you, he'll send a person? And when the devil wants to tempt you, he'll also send a person?" Not every man who walks into your life will be from God. No matter how lonely or desperate you feel, ask God to show you if someone was sent by him.

The devil will try to throw you off course right before you're about to receive God's best. Do not give up. Don't settle or give in to a guy who appears to be good.

Pray the prayer below, or pray what God is putting on your heart.

God, thank you for giving me authority and power to fight against the devil. Help me to stand strong in your power, and to declare your truth over every situation and temptation I face. In Jesus' name, amen.

WEEK 5 REFLECTION

Single & Faithful

Take some time to reflect and look back at how God spoke to you this past week. Journal your thoughts below, and consider answering the following questions:

- What key takeaways or revelations did you have this week?
- Which scriptures or Bible verses stuck out to you?
- What are you going to do differently moving forward after this week?

WEEK 5 REFLECTION

WEEK 6

God Writes the Best Love Stories

God Positions

"We can make our plans, but the Lord determines our steps."

Proverbs 16:9 NLT

I moved to San Diego to figure out what I was supposed to do with my life. While I prayed God would show me the career I should pursue, I wondered if I would meet my husband in Southern California.

For four years, I had lived in Chicago and hoped I would meet someone. But it didn't happen. Was moving across the country to meet my husband part of God's plan? What if he wasn't here? How and where would I meet him?

Moving to a new state was only the first step in God's plan to bring me and my future husband together. But I felt overwhelmed with all the decisions that came next. Which church was I supposed to go to? Should I join meetup groups for singles? And should I try online dating again?

Only God knew how I was going to meet my husband. But it was up to me to position myself where God was calling me to go.

Today, we're talking about how God positions us to meet our future spouse, and how to navigate all the questions that come up along the way.

Read Genesis 24:1-9. In Genesis 24:5, Abraham's servant responds after Abraham asks him to find a wife for Isaac. How do you think Abraham's servant felt after Abraham made this request?

Abraham gave his servant the most important task of his lifetime. I probably would have felt like I had been given an impossible task. The servant had to travel on foot to a foreign land to find a woman related to Abraham. They didn't have GPS back then. So how was the servant supposed to find Isaac a wife?

Since the servant worked for a man of faith like Abraham, he probably knew that all things are possible with God. Even finding a wife for his master's son was possible with the Lord.

Continue reading Genesis 24:10-27. How did the servant show his faith that God would come through?

The servant took action to set out on his journey, but he also prayed to God. He knew he could not accomplish this task without God's help. So he put his trust in the only person who could make his journey a success.

As the servant approached a well at his destination, God brought Rebekah to the scene before the servant had finished praying. If you read the rest of Isaac and Rebekah's love story in Genesis 24, you'll see that Rebekah became Isaac's wife and Isaac loved her deeply.

If this were a romance movie, this chapter in the Bible would have ended with, "And Rebekah became Isaac's wife, and they lived happily ever after." But if you've read the rest of their story, you know they had some family issues with their sons, Esau and Jacob. But that's a lesson for another Bible study.

What does God want to teach you through their love story? God positioned Isaac and Rebekah to meet in an unlikely way during an unlikely time. They didn't have dating apps or social media back then to find the perfect match. And they didn't even live in the same city. But God brought Rebekah to Isaac, and they loved each other.

Rebekah and Isaac's story is just one example of how God orchestrated people to meet in the Bible. If you remember Ruth's story from week 5, God brought her and Boaz together. Ruth could have worked in any field, but she found Boaz's field. Back then, it was dangerous for a woman to work alone. God brought Ruth to the field where she would be safe and meet her husband.

If God positioned these couples to meet back then, what makes you think he can't position you to meet your future husband? With your own love story, God knows exactly when you and your future husband will meet. He knows when you'll start dating, and when you'll get married.

Looking back at my love story, God did some serious orchestrating to bring me and my husband together. My husband is originally from Taiwan and I grew up in Michigan. God had lined things up for years for both of us to live in San Diego. And we faced big, life decisions along the way. Do I take that job? Which college should I attend? Should I transfer jobs and move across the country? Which church should I go to? And what volunteer team should I join?

I met my husband at church while serving on the same volunteer team. But before we met, God made sure we were in the same city, at the same church, and on the same team. Before I became a writer, I worked in public accounting for years. I didn't like accounting, so I didn't understand why God had me in that job. But God used that job to bring me out to San Diego where I met my husband.

As you pray and think about where you'll meet your husband, trust God to guide you. I don't know where you'll meet your future husband, or when you'll start dating. But God knows.

Do you think you are in the right place (city, church, career, etc.) to meet your future husband?

But where do most couples meet? What places should you consider as you pray about meeting your future spouse?

According to a study conducted by theknot.com[7] ("The Knot Survey"), most couples meet online, or through mutual friends. The Knot Survey found that about one in every four couples meet online, and about one in five couples meets through mutual friends.

Does this mean you should download the dating apps? Not necessarily. Just because one in four couples meets online doesn't mean you'll find your husband online. Pray and ask God if you should pursue online dating. If he puts it on your heart, don't let shame or judgment hold you back. But make sure it's something God wants you to pursue before you swipe left and right. If you don't have peace about it, don't do it.

I know several Christian couples who met online. As I talked about earlier in this study, I used dating apps before I had a relationship with Jesus. But online dating only made me feel worse about myself. When I asked God if I should download the apps again, I didn't have peace about it. I didn't have a desire to be on them, so I felt like God wasn't leading me down that path.

Outside of dating apps, how else could you meet your husband? According to The Knot Survey, about 19 percent of couples met through mutual friends, or where a friend introduced them. Keep this in mind when you're tempted to stay home when your friend invites you to a birthday party or church gathering.

When you're single, do not underestimate the connections you can make through a community of diverse people. If you don't enjoy hanging out with married couples, remember that they may know a single guy who could be a good fit. And that sweet old lady at church? Her grandson may be praying for a woman like you.

If you're praying for a godly man, pray and consider all opportunities to meet single men at your church. Your church community should be the first place you consider, since that's where most single Christian men gather. As you know, I met my husband at church, and I know several other couples that met in God's house.

But it's important to make sure you're at the right church, and that you're getting involved so you can meet people. Don't get frustrated when you don't meet a guy after attending a church service. You could meet a guy in the church lobby, but most couples meet by doing something they enjoy, or through a mutual friend. For example, you could meet your husband serving or volunteering like I did. Or you could meet a guy in a co-ed small group or Bible study. Find out all the co-ed ministries and groups your church has, and pray about each one.

You could also meet your husband doing things you enjoy, or through activities you do every week. What hobbies do you have? You could meet someone through a sports league, or a meetup group in your area. If you've been wanting to play beach volleyball or join a hiking group, go for it. You never know who you could meet.

Outside of your hobbies, think about the places you go to regularly. You could meet your husband through work, at the gym, or even your favorite coffee shop.

As you pray, trust God to guide you. Ask God if there is anything you need to pursue to position yourself to meet your future husband. You may not know how you could meet someone, but God is lining up every piece of your love story.

What has God put on your heart to pursue? Do you feel led to try online dating? Or to get involved at church or in your community to meet single men?

Pray the prayer below, or pray what God is putting on your heart.

God, thank you for writing my love story. I believe you are positioning me and my future husband to meet. If we haven't met yet, I pray you lead us towards each other. If we've already met, I pray you show us we're meant to get married. In Jesus' name, amen.

Stepping Out in Faith

"Faith without works is dead."

James 2:26 CSB

I sighed as I took my red, off-the-shoulder dress out of the closet. Another Valentine's Day single. My friend had invited me to a singles mixer hosted by our church, but I didn't want to go. I was grateful my church put on events for single people, but attending a mixer was the last thing I wanted to do on Valentine's Day.

I didn't feel like getting dressed up and putting myself out there. Attending these types of events hoping to meet a guy was exhausting. All I wanted to do was curl up on the couch in my coziest pajamas and eat mac-n-cheese while reading my new Christian fiction novel.

God already knew how I felt about dating. I had dated my fair share of wrong men in my twenties. And I didn't want to go on dates that didn't lead anywhere. A few times in prayer, I told God I didn't want a guy to ask me out if he wasn't my future husband. I didn't want to waste time dating men who weren't the one.

As I debated going to the mixer, I knew I needed to put myself out there. But I was involved at church and met new guys pretty often. Wasn't I doing enough? Or should I consider downloading the dating apps again?

In the end, my friend convinced me to go. "This is a great way to meet single guys, especially Christian men." I forced myself to smile as I stepped into the clubhouse where the mixer was held. I scanned the room. *God, when will I meet my husband? Is he here?*

Today, we're discussing the purpose of dating, and how much you should date as you trust God with your love story.

Read James 2:14-26.

Faith is a big part of our relationship with God. We are saved through faith in Jesus Christ, and we show faith in God through our actions. Think of all the people in the Bible who acted in great faith when others thought they were crazy. Noah built a boat before it started raining. Abraham left his family, even though he didn't know where he was going. Rahab risked her life to hide the spies before she discovered who God really was.

In the NLT translation of James 2:14, it says, "What good is it, dear brothers and sisters, if you say you have faith but don't show it by your actions?"

With dating and meeting your future husband, are you showing God that you have faith through your actions?

God calls us to walk by faith, and this applies to our dating life, too. If you're praying for God to move in other areas of your life, would you do your part and take action?

Suppose you're praying for God to reveal your unique purpose and calling, and you're asking God to show you the job he has for you. As you wait on God to bring you the right job, you step out in faith by doing research, going to networking events, updating your resume, and applying for jobs. You have faith that God will bring you the right job. But you know it takes work on your part.

Why is it so hard to exercise the same level of faith in dating? Just like it says in James 2, faith without works is dead, even when praying for a husband.

As you pray for a spouse, step out in faith and put yourself out there. Have you ever heard the expression, "God can't steer a parked car?" You can only steer a car when it's moving. God wants to direct you with dating, but he can't guide you if you don't get moving first.

Waiting on God for a husband does not mean you sit around and wait for your husband to show up on your doorstep. Unless your husband is the Amazon delivery guy, your husband will not show up at your door.

But is it the guy's job to find a wife? In Proverbs 18:22, it says, "A man who finds a wife finds a good thing." (CSB). Some women argue they don't have to worry about finding a husband. It's up to the man to find a wife.

While the man should be the pursuer in the relationship, a woman should not sit around expecting to be found. The key to waiting in faith is to let yourself be found.

Think about the places you go to most often. If you go to the same places every week, and you interact with the same people you already know, you have a slim chance of meeting your husband.

How could you switch up your routine to meet more single men? If you belong to a local church, attend a different service one week or attend a co-ed event that you haven't been to. If you attend a smaller church, pray and consider checking out another church in your area. Do your research online and look for churches that have events and ministries to interact with men.

Are you putting yourself out there for your husband to find you? How could you switch up your routine to meet more single men?

Going on dates is another way to show faith. But how do you know if you should date? And what's the purpose of dating?

Christians have mixed views on the purpose of dating. Some Christians believe that the end goal of dating is to get married. So you should only date people you could marry one day. Other Christians argue you need to date in order to get to know someone. How will you know if you want to marry someone if you don't get to know them? Some Christians also think that dating is a good way to discover what you like and don't like in a person. And just like a job interview, going on dates can help you practice, so you're more prepared when you date the right person.

Dating is essential if you want to meet your husband, but it's important to make sure you're dating for the right reasons. If you know you wouldn't marry someone, then there's no reason to date them. And if you're not ready to date and you're going on dates to make yourself feel better, this isn't fair to the other person.

Keep in mind that going on a date does not mean that you will marry that person. If a guy asks you out for coffee, don't start looking at wedding dresses. The purpose of a date is to get to know someone. Don't put too much pressure on the date, expecting that they'll become your husband.

But how many dates should you go on? Should you go on several dates every month if you want to meet your husband?

There is no magic formula for the number of dates you should go on. I have some friends who met their husband after dating all the Christian men in their city. But I have other friends who hardly dated before dating their husband.

Focus on quality rather than quantity when deciding how many dates you should go on. Would you rather go on fewer dates with men that are a good fit? Or would you rather waste time going on several dates with the wrong type of men?

You need to be open to dating to see if you're compatible with someone. But you don't have to date hundreds of men before finding the one. All it takes is meeting that one guy who will become your husband. If you're worried that you should date more, focus on where God is positioning you. If you're where God wants you to be and open to going on dates, then trust that you'll meet your future husband.

Dating requires time, energy, and commitment—it can feel like a part-time job. And since you're focused on what God has called you to as a single woman, there may be seasons where you aren't dating at all. And that's okay. Depending on your season, God may not want you to date right now. For example, maybe you're still getting rid of some of the baggage from your past, like we talked about in week 4. Or maybe God wants you to focus on your relationship with him before you're ready to date.

You'll have seasons where you're not focused on dating. And sometimes you may feel so frustrated that God wants you to take a break. But what's most important is that you're focusing on what God has called you to focus on, and that you're open to dating when God shows you it's time. We live in a hustle-and-bustle world, and it's easy to think you don't have time to date. But if finding a spouse is a priority to you, then putting yourself out there needs to be a priority too.

Do you feel ready to date? Is God calling you to focus on dating in this season? Or has God highlighted something through this study that he wants you to work on first?

Let's talk about physical attraction when dating. Should you go on a date with someone you aren't attracted to? What if he's not your type?

As we talked about earlier in this study, physical appearance is just one attribute of a person. Even though culture focuses on a person's looks, God looks at the heart. And you may think you know what your man should look like, but only God knows what you need. Unless God has revealed what your husband will look like, don't turn a guy down just because he isn't your ideal type.

If you aren't attracted to a guy right away, don't assume he's not the one. It's not always love at first sight, like in the movies. Even though I liked my husband right away, he didn't like me until a year later. And I know several couples who started out as friends first before they started dating.

Attraction can grow over time once you get to know someone. But if you've given a guy a chance and you're still not attracted to him? Don't force it. Remember, God intended for sex to be passionate between a husband and wife. And he wants you to be attracted to your spouse. Read Song of Solomon in the Bible if you're not convinced. Don't worry that you'll be forced to marry someone you aren't attracted to.

Pray the prayer below, or pray what God is putting on your heart.

God, I have faith that you're doing everything you can to bring me and my husband together. I will do my part and step out in faith. Show me how to put myself out there and trust you on this dating journey. In Jesus' name, amen.

Who Do You Want More?

"Seek the Kingdom of God above all else, and live righteously, and he will give you everything you need."

Matthew 6:33 NLT

My friend Emma and I were at women's prayer, and I noticed the familiar look of anxiety in my friend's eyes. "What do you need prayer for today?" I wrapped my arm around her.

Emma sighed. "I need prayer for my future husband. I've been asking God for clarity, but I need to know when we're going to meet." I closed my eyes. My heart broke for my friend. I knew how she felt about being single, but this was the fifth week in a row she was desperate for prayer for her future husband.

We had already prayed that God would bring her the right man. We already declared that God would confirm whether the guy she liked was the one. But this week, the Holy Spirit gave me the strength to speak the words God had put on my heart.

"Emma, we can pray for your future husband again, but that's not what you need prayer for." Emma brushed a stray tear from her face as I continued. "You need prayer to trust God, and to focus on him instead of your future husband." Emma nodded her head as she cried some more. I believed God would answer my friend's prayers for a husband, but I knew her obsession with meeting her spouse wasn't healthy.

Today, we're talking about how to make sure praying for your future husband doesn't become an idol.

Earlier in this study, we studied how Abraham waited for God to fulfill his promise through Isaac. Now, let's see what God told Abraham to do after Isaac was born.

Read Genesis 22:1-18. Why did God tell Abraham to sacrifice Isaac and then stop him at the last minute?

Can you imagine what Abraham was thinking? He is about a hundred years old at this point. After years of waiting, God told Abraham to kill the son who was supposed to fulfill God's promise. In Hebrews 11, the Bible shows us how Abraham felt through all of this.

Read Hebrews 11:17-19. What was Abraham thinking?

God tested Abraham to see if Abraham would obey him. Faith is important to God, but he also wants to make sure that he remains the number one person in our hearts. Even above the things we've waited so long for.

In Matthew 7:9-11, Jesus says God wants to give us good gifts as our heavenly Father. But he will give them to us when we're ready to receive them. He wants to make sure our hearts are in the right place. And God also wants to make sure the things we're believing for don't become an idol in our lives.

In Exodus 20:3-6, the Bible tells us that God is a jealous God, and that we must not have any other gods but God. And in Romans 1:19-23, God turned from people that worshipped the things he created instead of him.

When you desire a future husband more than God, this is an idol. Even if God gave you the man you've been praying for, your heart won't be in the right place to receive it. And it won't end well. When you receive something when your heart isn't ready, you can hold on too tight out of fear and can ruin the relationship.

Have you heard of a woman described as "too clingy"? Maybe you've heard a guy friend say he broke up with a girl because she was too clingy, or maybe you've been described this way. Women can get clingy when they become obsessed with being in a relationship. They've wanted a boyfriend for so long, but they're afraid of losing him. They compensate for their fear by controlling or smothering the relationship.

If you desire a guy more than God, you'll rely on your boyfriend to meet all your needs instead of God. Maybe you expect your boyfriend to solve all your problems. Or maybe you think you'll finally be happy once you're in a relationship. Making a man the center of your life will only set your relationship up for failure. Relying on a guy for everything puts too much pressure on him. No man is perfect, even if he is a Christian. And no man can replace God in your life.

Be honest with yourself. Are you desiring your future husband more than God? Have you been obsessing or idolizing meeting your future husband?

If you've been worried about meeting your future husband, how can you have peace as you wait on God? And how can you stop obsessing over meeting the man God has for you?

In Isaiah 26:3 NLT, it says, "You will keep in perfect peace all who trust in you, all whose thoughts are fixed on you!"

The more you shift your focus to God and remember what he is capable of, the more peace you'll have. Remember how we talked about how to have more trust in God back in week 3? When you feel anxious or worried about meeting your husband, remember what God has done for you. Remember all the miracles God has already performed in your life. The more you focus on God instead of your future husband, the more peace you'll have, knowing that God is in control.

As you trust God with your desire for marriage, how can you shift your focus more to him instead of your future husband?

Focusing on God not only gives you more peace as you wait for your prayers to be answered, but allows God to provide for you as your heavenly Father. When you're single, it's easier to trust God to provide for your basic needs. He provides the food you eat, the house you live in, and the clothes you wear. But why is it so hard to trust God with the one thing you want most?

If you're struggling to trust that God can provide a husband for you, pray and declare the verse below out loud.

"Seek the Kingdom of God above all else, and live righteously, and he will give you everything you need."

Matthew 6:33 NLT

Whenever I doubted whether God could bring me a husband, the Holy Spirit reminded me of Matthew 6:33. I was doing my part by seeking God first and walking in his ways. And now it was up to God to provide my every need, including my future husband. It wasn't up to me to go find one.

Over the last few weeks, we've studied how God provided for both Rahab and Ruth. They were both foreign women who did not grow up with God, but God provided their every need as they trusted him. If God provided a husband for both Ruth and Rahab, he's capable of bringing you a man, too.

Do you trust God to provide your every need, including a husband? Describe any areas where you're struggling to trust him.

As you pray for God to grant your desire for marriage, remember that God wants you to trust him with everything. He promises to provide your every need, including a husband. Like it says in Matthew 6:25-34, if God provides for the birds and cares so wonderfully for the flowers, why wouldn't God provide for you?

You are made in the image of God. You are his masterpiece, as his beloved daughter of God. And God delights in giving good gifts to his children. As you continue to pray for your future husband, remember that God wants to provide all your needs, including a godly husband.

Pray the prayer below, or pray what God is putting on your heart.

God, forgive me for obsessing or idolizing over my future husband. Help me desire and seek you first above anything else in my life. Thank you for providing all my needs as my heavenly Father, including my future husband. In Jesus' name, amen.

The Desires of Your Heart

***"Take delight in the Lord,
and he will give you your heart's desires."***

Psalm 37:4 NLT

When I first liked my husband, I wasn't sure if my desires were from God, or if I liked him because he was different. I had been used to worldly guys that didn't treat me with respect. So I wasn't sure if I liked Jeff just because he was one of the first Christian guys I met. He was an angel compared to all the men I had dated in the past. But did this mean he was the one?

My feelings for Jeff grew stronger, so I prayed for God to confirm the desires on my heart. And I prayed Jeff would ask me out.

But as months went on, Jeff still hadn't made a move. Were my desires from God? I had liked guys in the past and they weren't the one, so how was I to know whether Jeff was the one God had for me?

A few of my other friends also prayed for their future spouse. But some worried that marriage wasn't in God's plans for them. They had been praying and walking in God's ways for years. But God hadn't brought them a husband yet.

As you pray in faith, how do you know if your desire for marriage is from God? And when you like someone, how do you know whether these desires are from God?

Today, we're talking about how God grants the desires of our heart. Specifically, how to make sure we align our desires with God's desires for our lives.

Write out Psalm 37:4.

Write out Philippians 2:13.

In Matthew 7:7-11, Jesus tells us God delights in giving good gifts to his children, and that we should seek and ask God for what we want through prayer. But how do you know if what you're asking for is God's will for your life? And if your desires are from God, why hasn't he granted these desires yet?

Psalm 37:4 is a popular Bible verse that gets used out of context. Some Christians argue God will grant the desires on their heart because he's a good heavenly Father. While others argue God isn't a magic genie who will grant whatever we ask for. And some people claim that if they have a desire to do something, then it must be from God.

In Galatians 5:16-26, the Bible talks about the battle between the desires of our flesh and the Spirit. "For the flesh desires what is against the Spirit, and the Spirit desires what is against the flesh; these are opposed to each other, so that you don't do what you want." (Galatians 5:17 CSB)

The Bible provides examples of desires of the flesh vs. the Spirit. Desires of the flesh include: sexual immorality, moral impurity, promiscuity, idolatry, jealousy, envy, drunkenness, and several others. Desires of the Spirit are described in Galatians 5:22-23. "But the fruit of the Spirit is love, joy, peace, patience, kindness, goodness, faithfulness, gentleness, and self-control." (CSB)

Not every desire we have is from God. What our body wants will often differ from what the Spirit wants. For example, maybe you have the desire to watch porn, or to starve yourself because you don't like how your body looks. These are desires of the flesh that are not from God.

How many guys have you liked where you thought they could be the one? But then you realized they were definitely not the man God has for you. I thought I liked several men before I married my husband. But my feelings were built on lust and the longing to be in a relationship.

Have you ever liked someone, or had a desire to do something that you knew wasn't from God?

As I prayed over the specific desires on my heart, God clarified how he would grant my desires. When we surrender our desires to God and delight in him, he will give us his desires for our life. We see this concept in Philippians 2:13, where it says, "For God is working in you, giving you the desire and the power to do what pleases him." (NLT)

Have you ever had a random desire to do something for God? Or has a desire ever gone away after surrendering it to him? Your desires for your life probably changed when you first gave your life to Jesus. And as you walk with God, he will put new desires on your heart to make an impact for his kingdom. When you surrender your life and desires to God, he will put his desires for your life on your heart.

But what does take delight in the Lord mean? God wants us to come to him out of love, not when we want something. When he sees that your heart is in the right place, God can trust you with the plans he has for you. And he will grant the desires he puts on your heart.

As I prayed for my desires for Jeff, I declared Psalm 37:4 and Philippians 2:13 over myself. I prayed that if these desires weren't from God, that he would take them away. I asked God to give me his desires for my life, and I surrendered my desires for Jeff to God.

As you surrender your desire for marriage, it's important to obey God even if you don't like what he says. Surrendering is being willing to give up your desires, no matter what God says. It's asking God to close the doors that need to be closed, instead of just asking God to give you what you want. And surrendering your desires means letting God give you his desires for your life, instead of asking God to bless the desires you already have.

For example, if you really like a guy, you've probably asked God to confirm if he's the one. But if you've already decided in your heart that you're going to stay with him, even if God says no, this isn't surrender. This is putting your own desires above God's.

Have you fully surrendered your desire for marriage to God? If you like someone, are you willing to obey God, even if God says he's not the one?

But how do you know if God's plans for you include marriage? What if God is calling you to a life of singleness?

My friend, if you've asked yourself this question, you are not alone. I asked this question myself when God wasn't confirming the desires on my heart. And I know several women who wonder if marriage isn't God's plan since it hasn't happened yet.

If you're doubting whether God is calling you to get married, continue to surrender your desires to him. Trust that the Holy Spirit will guide you. God calls the majority of people to be married. Remember, God said in Genesis 2:18 that it is not good for man to be alone.

And don't be shy to keep praying and asking God for a husband. Some women are afraid to ask for a husband because they don't know if it's God's will. They don't want to believe or hope for something that isn't from God. But remember, God wants us to pray and ask for the desires on our heart. And when you surrender your desires to him, you can trust that he will align your desires with his.

If God's plans for you don't include a husband, he will let you know. Trust that if he's calling you to a life of singleness, that his plans for you are even better than marriage. I know that's hard to believe right now, but God knows the plans he has for your life. And he promises to give you hope and a future, even if it doesn't include marriage.

Has God changed any of your desires during this Bible study? Write the desires you have about marriage, or for a specific guy you've been praying about.

Pray the prayer below, or pray what God is putting on your heart.

God, I surrender my desire for marriage to you. Thank you for aligning my desires with the desires you have for my life. If a desire is not from you, make it clear. In Jesus' name, amen.

God Confirms

"I will instruct you and teach you in the way you should go; I will counsel you with my loving eye on you."

Psalm 32:8 NIV

I had liked this guy at church for almost a year now, and I kept asking God the same question in prayer. "God, is Jeff the one? If he's the guy I'm supposed to marry, confirm it."

Since I had liked Jeff for so long, I thought he was my future husband. I had prayed that God would give me his desires for my life. And since my desires didn't go away, maybe Jeff was the one. I was so convinced, that I even wrote a few letters starting with, "Dear Jeff, my future husband..."

But on the days Jeff didn't show any interest in me, I thought maybe he wasn't the one. I even left church in tears a few times because he didn't talk to me. *God, please confirm if he's my husband. I don't want to like him if he's not the one.*

I still hoped Jeff could be my future husband, but how was I to know for sure? How would God confirm it? And why wasn't God speaking to me after liking him for so long?

On the last day of this Bible study, we're studying how God speaks, and how he confirms his will for our lives through the Holy Spirit.

Read John 14:15-17 and John 14:22-27. Which names does Jesus use to describe the Holy Spirit?

Read John 16:5-15. How does Jesus describe the Holy Spirit's purpose? Describe the roles or functions the Holy Spirit performs in our lives. Hint: pay attention to all the verbs listed in these scriptures.

Understanding who the Holy Spirit is and his function is essential to hearing God's voice. The trinity of God consists of God, Jesus, and the Holy Spirit. Depending on which church you attended growing up, you may not have heard about the Holy Spirit. In John 14 and 16, Jesus gives his last farewell teachings to his disciples before he was crucified. Since this is one of his last teachings, Jesus shows us that the Holy Spirit plays an important role in our lives.

The Holy Spirit serves many purposes, but he primarily acts as our counselor and spirit of truth. When we accept Jesus as our Lord and Savior, the Holy Spirit makes his home inside us. He wants to guide us and teach us God's truth. In John 16, Jesus also tells us that the Holy Spirit will convict us and declare what is to come. A conviction is when God corrects you, or tells you he doesn't like something in your life. For example, if you've been dating the wrong type of men, the Holy Spirit has probably convicted you through this Bible study. And convictions are a good thing! It means God has already been speaking to you.

God also tells us several times in the Bible that he will guide us and direct our steps. In Psalm 32:8 NLT, God says, "I will guide you along the best pathway for your life. I will advise you and watch over you." In Proverbs 3:5-6 NLT, it says, "Trust in the Lord with all your heart; do not depend on your own understanding. Seek his will in all you do, and he will show you which path to take."

Can God show you the man you're supposed to marry? Yes. He wants to guide you through the Holy Spirit. Who you marry is the second biggest decision you'll make after choosing to follow Jesus. God wants you to end up with the right person just as much as you do. He already knows who you're going to marry, and you can trust that he'll confirm who your husband is.

God promises to guide us, but how does the Holy Spirit speak to us? How do we know when God is confirming his will?

If you want to hear God's voice, you need a heart posture to obey him, even if you don't like the answer. Author Priscilla Shirer talks about hearing God's voice in her Bible study, *Discerning the Voice of God*[8]. Deciding in advance to obey God is the key to hearing God's voice. If he already knows you will not obey him, why would he speak to you?

Below are examples of how the Holy Spirit speaks, and how God can confirm who you're supposed to marry. The Holy Spirit may speak to you in a few different ways, or he may only speak in one way to confirm his will.

Peace

The Holy Spirit often guides us through peace. In 1 Corinthians 14:33 ESV, the Bible says, "For God is not a God of confusion but of peace." In 2 Corinthians 2:12-13, the Holy Spirit directed Paul on his travels through peace. "... even though the Lord opened a door for me, I had no rest in my spirit because I did not find my brother Titus." (CSB)

If you don't have peace or rest in your Spirit about a guy, he may not be the one. Or it may not be the right time. A guy may check all the right boxes on paper, but if you don't have peace about him, pray into it. God may be telling you he isn't your husband.

A Strong Assurance or Knowing

You may know the Holy Spirit is speaking to you when you have a strong assurance, knowing, or feeling about something. When the Holy Spirit is trying to get your attention, it may also feel like your heart is on fire, or like your body is lit up with excitement. In Pastor Jentezen Franklin's book, *Right People, Right Place, Right Plan*[9], he describes it as, "When the Holy Spirit speaks, His voice comes with a power that grips you."

In Luke 24:32, two disciples realized Jesus was walking with them when their hearts burned within them. "They said to each other, 'Weren't our hearts burning within us while he was talking with us on the road and explaining the Scriptures to us?'" (CSB)

Some people use the expression, "When you know, you know" or, "I had a gut feeling." This is the Holy Spirit giving you a strong assurance or knowing about a decision.

A Voice from Within

When God speaks to us, he rarely speaks in an audible voice. But his voice feels like a whisper from inside of us. When Elijah sought the Lord's voice in 1 Kings 19:12, God spoke to him in a whisper.

I've never heard God speak in an audible voice, but I've heard a voice speak to me from within. This feels more like a vivid thought, or an urgent thought that came out of nowhere. Or sometimes it feels like a whisper on my heart.

Scriptures in God's Word

The Holy Spirit often speaks to us while reading scriptures in the Bible. In Psalm 119:105 NLT, it says, "Your word is a lamp to guide my feet and a light for my path." God also tells us in Hebrews 4:12 NLT that "... the word of God is alive and powerful. It is sharper than the sharpest two-edged sword."

When God speaks to you, it may feel like a verse or passage is highlighted, or like it's jumping off the page. It can also feel like a scripture speaks to your heart, and was exactly what you needed to hear in that moment.

No scripture in the Bible will explicitly tell you who your future husband is. But don't underestimate how God wants to speak to you about dating through scripture. The Bible is full of verses and stories that you can apply to your life as you pursue marriage. But you have to take the time to study what God has already told you in his Word. God will also not tell you to do something that contradicts his Word. If you've been asking if you should marry a guy even though he's a nonbeliever, God already told you no. (See day 5 in week 1 if you need a reminder.)

Visions or Dreams

God can also speak through visions or dreams. In Acts 2:17 NLT, it says, "'In the last days,' God says, 'I will pour out my Spirit upon all people. Your sons and daughters will prophesy. Your young men will see visions, and your old men will dream dreams.'"

Visions occur when we are awake, where we visually see a picture in our mind of something. God speaks to us in dreams when we are asleep. Whenever you have a vision or dream, pray and ask the Holy Spirit to confirm if it was from God. Ask him to reveal what the vision or dream means.

Prophecies or Words of Knowledge

God also speaks through other people using prophecies or words of knowledge. In 2 Peter 1:20-21 NLT, it says "... You must realize that no prophecy in Scripture ever came from the prophet's own understanding, or from human initiative. No, those prophets were moved by the Holy Spirit, and they spoke from God."

The Holy Spirit can reveal what is to come through a prophecy, or give someone insight about you through a word of knowledge. Whenever someone tells you they have a prophecy or word from God for you, take it to God in prayer and ask him to confirm whether it was from him.

External Signs

God can also speak through external signs. In Judges 6, God already told Gideon to fight the Midianites, but Gideon wanted to make sure God was speaking to him. Gideon lays out a fleece and asks God to prove that it was him.

God may use external signs as a confirmation, but it's important not to rely on signs alone to confirm whether something is from God. Since you have direct access to him through the Holy Spirit, why would God want you to rely on external confirmations?

If you've been asking God to confirm whether a guy is your husband, don't expect the clouds to form a big 'YES' or 'NO' in the sky. He's already given you a counselor to guide you, and wants you to turn to the Holy Spirit when seeking God's will.

Based on how the Holy Spirit can speak, how has God been speaking to you about who you should date or marry?

God didn't confirm Jeff was my husband until we started dating. Once Jeff asked me out, all the prayers I prayed for a year were answered. Jeff pursued me with intention and made it clear he wanted to be my boyfriend. I also had a strong sense of peace and assurance about the relationship. Jeff also asked God to confirm whether I was the one. God confirmed I was his wife through a dream and prophecies that others had spoken over him.

Pray the prayer below.

God, thank you for speaking to me through the Holy Spirit. Thank you for guiding me as I date and step out in faith to meet my husband. And thank you for confirming the man you have for me. In Jesus' name, amen.

WEEK 6 REFLECTION

God Writes the Best Love Stories

Take some time to reflect and look back at how God spoke to you this past week. Journal your thoughts below, and consider answering the following questions:

- What key takeaways or revelations did you have this week?
- Which scriptures or Bible verses stuck out to you?
- What are you going to do differently moving forward after this week?

WEEK 6 REFLECTION

Note to Reader

Congrats! You just finished this 6-week Bible study! I'm so proud of you for sticking with it, and for inviting God to minister to your heart. Trusting God with your love story is not easy. But I pray and believe that God is already performing miracles to bring you and your future husband together.

If you enjoyed this Bible study, would you let me know? You saw how God spoke to me when I was single, and I would love to hear how God spoke to you through these pages.

Writing a review on Amazon is one of the best ways to share how this study encouraged you. Sharing a review on Amazon also helps more single women discover the book. God wants to reach ladies all over the world through this study, but I need your help spreading the word. Even short reviews on Amazon help, so thank you in advance for taking the time to write a review!

You can also email me at erinelisekiu@funandholy.com to share how God moved through this study. Don't forget to reach out when you and your future husband get engaged! I can't wait to see all the romantic engagement and wedding pics :)

If you have a friend who needs to experience God through this book, tell her about it or buy her a copy. If you have a group of friends that need a reminder that God is writing their love story, consider leading a group Bible study. Check out free resources for Bible study leaders at www.funandholy.com/biblestudy.

Wondering what to do next? Follow me on Instagram @erinelisekiu for more encouragement and Christian dating advice. You can also explore the Fun & Holy blog at www.funandholy.com for biblical answers to tough dating questions.

With Love,

Erin Elise Kiu

Free Resources at Fun & Holy

Are You Praying for a Husband?

FREE 14-Day Future Husband Prayer Challenge

www.funandholy.com/prayerchallenge

Are You Ready for a Relationship?

Take the Quiz
Personalized Dating Roadmap

www.funandholy.com/quiz

www.funandholy.com

Are You Struggling to Live for God in the World's Hookup Culture?

A CHRISTIAN FICTION NOVEL BY ERIN ELISE KIU BASED ON HER TESTIMONY

If you're struggling to break free from the hookup culture or dating the wrong men, this is the book for you my friend.

www.funandholy.com/books

Do You Need a Reminder That God Is Writing Your Love Story?

SCRIPTURE CARDS FOR SINGLE LADIES

Declare God's Word to renew your faith
30 scriptures related to singleness & dating
Over 90 positive declarations to pray over yourself & your future husband

www.funandholy.com/scripturecards

Acknowledgments

To the Holy Spirit, thank you for downloading this Bible study into my heart. Thank you for speaking to every woman who reads this book. You are doing even more than I can imagine, and I thank you for all the breakthrough and transformations that have already taken place.

To my husband, Jeff Kiu, thank you for letting God write our love story. Thank you for showing me that the Ephesians 5 type of love is possible in marriage. Thank you for cooking dinner and for helping me clean when I had the ladies over for Bible study. And thank you for holding me and speaking God's Word over me on the days I wanted to give up.

To my parents, Kathy and Dirk, thank you for believing in the dreams God has put on my heart to become a writer. Thank you for teaching me to swing hard, and not to underestimate what God wants to do through my life.

To my in-laws, Richard and Jane, thank you for welcoming me into the Kiu family with open hearts and open arms. To Mama, thank you for playing such a pivotal role in my love story, and for encouraging Jeff to pray and ask me out.

To the beta reader team who was the first to go through this study—Katy, Melody, Kristina, Angie, Rachel, Laura, Hollie, Angela, Rayna, Jess, Miriam, and Cambria—thank you for opening your hearts through this study. Thank you for sharing how God spoke to you, and for being vulnerable to talk about the not-so-fun parts about being single. Thank you for encouraging me when I felt like giving up, and for believing in all the women God will reach through this study. I look forward to celebrating your love stories at fun and holy bachelorette parties, and dancing at your weddings :)

To my mentors and leaders at Awaken Church in San Diego, thank you for empowering me to live out my God-given destiny in this crazy world. To Raechelle Rodriguez, thank you for believing in me and for reminding me of what's possible with God. To my lead pastors Leanne Matthesius and Becky Heinrichs, thank you for encouraging me to use my voice for the next generation. Thank you for modeling how to be both fun and holy so other women can experience the love of Jesus in this world.

To my fellow authors and writers from the Believe Conference—Charity, Angie, Jessica, Morgan, Kaelin, Stefanie, Carolyn, Ashlyn, and Brianna—thank you so much for all your encouragement and prayers on this writing journey. God ordained us all to meet through Karen Kingsbury's conference, and I believe God is moving through each one of us to get our stories into the world.

And a special shoutout to the Bible study author that God used to change my life—Priscilla Shirer. I haven't met you in person yet, and you probably don't know who I am. But thank you for obeying God's call to write *Discerning the Voice of God*. I surrendered my life to Jesus while doing that Bible study. My dream to write Bible studies was born shortly after. Thank you for inspiring me to write this study for God's daughters, and for showing me how the Holy Spirit can move through a Bible study.

Endnotes

Week 1

1. Definition of "Lust", *Merriam-Webster,* accessed on July 29, 2022, available online via https://www.merriam-webster.com/dictionary/lust.
2. Timothy Keller, *The Meaning of Marriage* (New York: Penguin Books, 2011).
3. Jim Stovall, "Horse Sense", *Timmaurer.com*, January 16, 2012, accessed on July 25, 2022, available online at https://timmaurer.com/2012/01/16/horse-sense/

Week 2

4. Definition of "Insecurity", *Dictionary.com*, accessed on July 29, 2022, available online via https://www.dictionary.com/browse/insecurity.
5. Annie F. Downs, "Episode 312: Q&A – Singleness", *That Sounds Fun Podcast with Annie F. Downs,* August 18 2021, available at https://www.anniefdowns.com/podcast/tsf-qa-singleness/.

Week 4

6. Michael Todd & Transformation Church, "There's No Condom For Your Heart // Relationship Goals Reloaded (Part 9) (Michael Todd)", *YouTube.com*, July 19, 2020, available online via https://www.youtube.com/watch?v=-UzJtFRnhr0.

Week 6

7. Esther Lee, "Dating Apps Are Officially the Most Popular Way to Meet a Spouse", *theknot.com*, Updated on October 30, 2019, available online via https://www.theknot.com/content/online-dating-most-popular-way-to-meet-spouse#:~:text=Online%20dating%20statistics%20reveal%20the,now%20officially%20through%20dating%20apps.&text=According%20to%20The%20Knot%202019,Tinder%2C%20Hinge%20and%20Bumble).

8. Priscilla Shirer, *Discerning the Voice of God: How to Recognize When God Speaks* (Nashville, TN: LifeWay Press, 2017) 8-13.

9. Jentezen Franklin, *Right People, Right Place, Right Plan: Discerning the Voice of God* (New Kensington, PA: Whitaker House, 2017).

Printed in Dunstable, United Kingdom

71674767R00123